£5·75B2

PASSING FOR WHITE

PASSING FOR WHITE

A study of racial assimilation in
a South African school

Graham Watson
PREFACE BY H. J. SIMONS

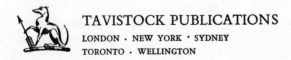

TAVISTOCK PUBLICATIONS
LONDON · NEW YORK · SYDNEY
TORONTO · WELLINGTON

First published in 1970
by Tavistock Publications Limited
11 New Fetter Lane, London E.C.4
Printed in Great Britain
in 11 point Bembo
by The Camelot Press Ltd, London and Southampton

SBN 422 73340 7
© *Graham Watson 1970*

Distributed in the USA
by Barnes & Noble Inc.

Contents

Preface

Most sociological works on South Africa are segmentary, being focused on the internal arrangements of a particular ethnic group rather than on its place in the wider society. Though valuable, and an indispensable source of information on social trends, these monographs tell us little about the social structure and the relations between its parts. That kind of insight must come from cross-sectional surveys such as Professor Watson has described in his important and fascinating account of the interactions between White and Coloured in a Cape Town working-class district.

He began his research with the hope that he would circumvent the vexatious, conscience-disturbing area of race relations by concentrating on a White school in a White neighbourhood. He soon discovered, however, that race and colour were dominant factors in his field. The school was located in a 'mixed' residential area inhabited by White and Coloured families of much the same social class. Though officially reserved for Whites, it included a significant number of Coloured pupils who 'passed' as White. Teachers, pupils, parents, and educational authorities could not escape the dilemmas that resulted from the tenacious and often successful attempts of light-skinned Coloured to improve their status by crossing the colour line.

Social mobility is much the same thing, whether it occurs between classes or between colour groups. To be accepted, the climber must adopt the habits, style of life, and attitudes of the group to which he aspires. In the case of the Coloured, it is also necessary that they should look like Whites. Appearance is largely, though not wholly, determined by birth, meaning ancestry; but the cultural traits of Whites are acquired, usually in stages, as the would-be 'pass-White' painfully edges his way into the White group. His occupation and income must be appropriate to the status of Whites; he must live in a White area, belong to a White church and social club, and obtain recognition as a White. He may then possibly qualify for a White identity card by reason of his appearance and associations, which are the determinants of White or Coloured status when evidence of ancestry is lacking or uncertain.

The number of identified, catalogued Coloured is close on two million; but the four million persons who are listed as Whites certainly include many with Coloured or African or Indian ancestry which, in strict biological terms, identifies them as Coloured. Professor Watson amply demonstrates, however, that racial identity, like kinship, is a sociological rather than a biological concept. Then borderlines between White and Coloured and between Coloured and African are sufficiently imprecise to permit some persons who were born into one category to pass into another. Hence it is possible for an individual to be classed as Coloured or African while his blood-relations – sibling, or parent, uncle or aunt – are classed as White or Coloured as the case may be.

A large bureaucracy is employed to stop this process, first by allocating people to their proper categories, and then by closing the loopholes through which individuals attempt to escape into a higher status group. The statutory and administrative controls are complicated and cumbersome. They include the amendment of the original entry in respect of race on any birth certificate, the reclassification of persons after due inquiry, and a right of appeal to a population registration board and the supreme court. The reclassification may involve the transfer of persons from the Coloured group to the White group, from White to Coloured, from Coloured to African, or from African to Coloured. In spite of this vigilance, the Minister of the Interior said in 1967 that there had been a 'gradual, but nevertheless, to my mind, dangerous integration of whites and non-whites'.

The Population Registration Amendment Act of 1967 introduced new tests to be used in race classification. A person must be classified as Coloured if both his parents were so classified, or if one was classified as White and the other as Coloured or African. If a person claiming to be White cannot prove that both his parents were so classified, the competent authorities are directed to take into account his habits, education, speech, and deportment; and to establish whether he is generally accepted as White, where he resides, works, and mixes socially with other members of the public.

White attitudes towards an aspiring pass-White may therefore have a decisive effect on his status. Professor Watson explains in a finely drawn analysis how the aspirant can manipulate the situation to his advantage by obtaining recognition as a White in a series of different roles, each of which involves the making of an *ad hoc* decision by a White. The latter may be the manager of a cinema, a bus conductor, the registrar of a hospital, a landlord, employer, church minister, a school principal, or School Board. When *ad hoc* decisions cumulatively favour the upward mobility of the aspirant, 'they constitute a process – that process which enables some Coloured persons to change their status to that of White persons'.

The decisions are usually motivated by self-interest, though this may amount to no more than reluctance to be involved in an embarrassing argument over the identity of a person who may in fact have White status. Material benefits are often at stake, however, as when employers rate skill and competence higher than genealogy. Interests may conflict, as in the school situation, which Professor Watson dissects with great skill and understanding. The principal fears that the school will be down-graded, either because of a decline in the number of pupils or because of an excessive number of pass-Whites among the pupils. He can enrol the prescribed quota by admitting pupils with Coloured ancestry, but then runs the risk that the school will be reclassified as Coloured.

The education authorities are exposed to conflicting pressures. An aspiring pass-White who wants his child to be admitted to a White school will canvass for the support of members of the School Committee and School Board. Contrary pressures come from White racists, perhaps also from disgruntled Coloured, who urge that pass-White children should be excluded from the school. A third factor is the bureaucracy, which is committed to implement the official policy of preventing the integration of Coloured and White.

An aspiring pass-White can hardly hope to escape these hazards without the support, active or passive, of his neighbours. The least they must do is to tolerate his presence in the local church, public house, cinema, or football club. It is only with their connivance that he can claim White status on the grounds of association and acceptance.

Contrary to apartheid dogmas and the opinion of most commentators, Professor Watson found that this support was forthcoming, that relations between White and Coloured residents were generally cordial. Both groups belonged to the artisan and semi-skilled class of workers, did the same kind of work for the same kind of pay, belonged to the same religious sects, and had the same prejudices. Both rejected Africans and were rejected in turn by more prosperous Whites, who looked down on the whole neighbourhood and regarded it as wholly Coloured. Left to themselves, without the intervention of the State and of racist parties, White and Coloured workers would probably develop a class-consciousness rather than a colour-consciousness.

To appreciate the significance of this hypothesis, one needs to recognize how difficult it is to put South Africa's social structure into any of the pigeon-holes that sociologists use to classify societies. The system itself can be described without great difficulty, since it is notorious, gross, and well documented. Few countries have received so much adverse attention abroad, few have been so vigorously and persistently attacked in international councils. Not many literate people anywhere can be quite oblivious to the enormities committed in the name of apartheid, the humiliations and injustices of compulsory racial discrimination, or the repressive measures used to keep Whites in the saddle. The elusive quality in the society is taxonomic and morphological, rather than functional.

None of the words commonly used to describe social strata quite fits the South African situation. There are classes, in both the Marxist and the Weberian sense, but government policy, legislation, and enforced segregation inhibit the growth of class-consciousness and solidarity between persons belonging to different ethnic groups. As Professor Watson has shown, White and Coloured workers are not able to interact and associate in freedom from State intervention. This is true also, to an even greater extent, of the relations between African and White workers. The class segments consequently terminate at the boundaries of each colour group, and reinforce racial exclusiveness at the expense of class solidarity.

For such reasons some sociologists think that caste is a more appropriate term than class to describe the hierarchical structure of South African society. They claim that its institutions of racial endogamy, work classification according to colour, and segregation resemble aspects of India's caste system. Professor Watson's findings disprove this hypothesis. Individual mobility is more pronounced in the South African system; its concepts of pollution and purity are enforced by statutory sanctions, rather than by religion; while the upper castes of India never had as much power and authority as are vested in the White oligarchy. It is unlikely that they will grow under the conditions of industrialization and economic integration.

There may be a simple explanation of this classificatory problem. The society itself is in a state of flux, and has no clear concept of itself or its destination. South Africans generally, in my opinion, are confused about their collective roles and the nature of their society. They are not allowed to recognize and act upon common interests that stretch across ethnic divisions; nor are they encouraged to think of themselves as members of a single national entity. There is no image with which all can identify, yet all are members of a single and integrated society. Their uncertainty stems from a schizophrenic cleavage between the contrived, rigid segregation structure and the living reality of social and economic integration.

Schizophrenics, whether individuals or collectivities, should be aided and encouraged to recognize the schism within them, and to substitute reality for myth and illusion. Regarded from this viewpoint, Professor Watson's book is therapeutic, and should be read widely by South Africans. It is a mirror in which they will get a glimpse of their true selves.

H. J. SIMONS

Lusaka
21 January 1970

INTRODUCTION

As early as 1932 Waller, in his as yet unrivalled study of schools as organizations, argued persuasively that the vulnerability of schools to environmental pressures intimately affects their structures.[1] His thesis has gained widespread acceptance, but it has not received as much attention as it merits. Of the 109 works cited in Bidwell's masterly review and bibliography of the sociology of education, a mere eleven are listed as dealing directly with school community relations.[2] Floud and Halsey, in their excellent bibliography of 762 works in the sociology of education, list a mere nineteen under the rubric of 'schools in relation to society and community'.[3] This book contributes towards a redressing of the balance. An attempt is made to relate the social structure of Colander High School, Cape Town, to the *racial* policy of the central government, the *racial* culture of the people of Colander, and the occupational ambitions of *race*-conscious school teachers. Description proceeds from a broad overview of *race* relations in Colander to a portrayal of the high school as a facilitating mechanism in the process of *passing for White*, and thence to a discussion of the effects of this involvement on the formal and informal structure of the teaching staff. Data collected, mainly by means of observer participation, in Colander and in the school are adduced in support of the argument.

Frequent allusions are made to Nature by propagandists of apartheid; but the division of mankind into races is an invention not of Nature but of Man. Races and the divisions which exist among them in South Africa reveal the hidden hand of nothing more elemental than the bureaucracy of Pretoria. If this is kept firmly in mind, there is no cause for bewilderment in the facts that brothers and sisters can belong to different *races*, that *White* adults can start life as *Coloured* children, that men can live as *Coloureds* but work as *Whites*. It happens quite often.

Those who at some stage of their lives have been Coloured – in South Africa the term denotes those of mixed White and non-White ancestry – but who, by subterfuge, have subsequently succeeded in being accepted as White are known as *pass-Whites*. Whites know little about them, and the secrecy which envelops the process of passing ensures that this will always be so.[4] I came to know of them for a variety of reasons, including, ironically, a determination to avoid embarking upon a study that would inevitably involve race relations. Like many of my fellow students at the University of Cape Town, I was appalled by the inane racism espoused by my White compatriots but, unlike some, later to suffer imprisonment and torture for their convictions, I felt there was nothing to be done and preferred not to be brought face to face with the palpable effects of apartheid. That meant confining my research to the White community. Having worked as a part-time school-teacher, I had developed an interest in schools, and what could be further from the study of race-relations than research into the social organization of a White urban high school? So I attempted to interest school principals in the proposal. It is no accident that Mr Jones, Principal of the pseudonymous Colander High, was the only one willing to help. He had his reasons. The grades his pupils obtained in public examinations were extraordinarily poor and the Cape Provincial Department of Education had demanded an explanation. Mr Jones saw me as a kind of social worker who would inform the Department of just how lacking was the home background whence the pupils came, thus exonerating himself and his teachers of blame. After teaching at the school for some months, I realized that the home background to which Mr Jones referred was often Coloured. A sizeable proportion of the adolescent boys and girls of this purportedly all-White South African school were pass-Whites. Nobody could have been more astonished – or dismayed – at the ironic discovery than I.

'We want no mixing of languages, no mixing of cultures, no mixing of religions, and no mixing of races'[5] is a statement which accurately reflects the philosophy embodied in the plethora of legislation affecting schooling in South Africa. White children must, by law, attend schools reserved for Whites only and must secure instruction through the medium of the mother tongue, be it Afrikaans (the language of the Afrikaner White majority) or English, and Coloured children must attend Coloured schools. Yet, twenty years after the nakedly racist Nationalist Party came to power, there still exists in the land of apartheid a number of public schools, reserved by law for Whites of English mother-tongue, which contain a considerable proportion of swarthy pass-White pupils of Afrikaans extraction. Colander High School is by no means unique.

To understand how this can be, it is necessary to consider the White and Coloured people of Colander and the relations that obtain between them, to examine the nature of passing for White, to recount the history of racially mixed schooling in South Africa,[6] and to lay bare the motivations of White school principals in knowingly admitting non-White pupils to their schools: all that is done in the earlier chapters of this book.

To arrive at such an understanding is not the sole purpose of the book. Research was begun with the intention of describing and analysing the social organization of a high school, a field of research conveniently neglected by educational sociologists. This description and analysis takes up the latter chapters.

The two halves of the book are closely interrelated. The examination of the social organization of Colander High School revealed certain eccentricities: friction between teachers and pupils, the pre-eminence of the class as a unit of social organization, a rapid turnover of recruits, a remarkable cleavage between long-term teachers and tiros, and conflict between Principal and Vice-Principal. It is in an attempt to account for these eccentricities that the school is viewed in its social context.

At this point it would be as well to say something about the technique of study.

The social structure of the school could almost have been especially constructed to confound the inquirer. A school depends very largely upon its reputation for the quantity and quality of its intake of both staff and pupils. Outsiders, free of the subtle informal pressures which teachers can bring to bear on their fellows, cannot be relied upon to gloss over facts which do not reflect to the school's credit. Hence the elaborate whiting of the sepulchre on visits from Inspectors; and hence also the evasive manner, often amounting to suspicion and downright hostility, with which the researcher is greeted. If teachers are not ready to treat the outsider with candour, still less are the bureaucrats of the school system. They are sensitive to the complaints of parents, many of whom feel that even the most impersonal and superficial investigation of their children is an unwarranted intrusion on their privacy. The outsider is free to ask questions, and many do; but all they get is answers. To get more than answers the outsider himself must become part of the school. He must, in other words, adopt the technique of investigation known as observer participation, a technique that was employed throughout this study. I spent an academic year teaching at Colander High School, on a part-time basis, and have since frequently visited the school over a period of many months. Some of these months were spent living within two hundred yards of the school buildings.

Just as it was necessary to adopt the technique of observer participation in the school, so was it necessary to adopt the same technique in the community which the school serves. Government officials have, in recent times, made house-to-house visits in Colander in an effort to classify the inhabitants into various ethnic groups and to prevent social mobility among them. Such visits have, not unnaturally, aroused a great deal of resentment and hostility. This hostility is visited upon anyone who tours the area armed with pencil and questionnaire: who knows? they might be government officials. So the sociologist cannot with confidence ask even the simplest of questions: he cannot ask a respondent where he or his siblings grew up, went to school, or goes to work; for each of these questions, if truthfully answered, elicits information which provides a clue to the ethnicity of the respondent and his siblings. The sociologist is therefore left with no choice – it is observer participation or nothing.

The social configuration of Colander might be thought to lend itself to the social survey, to the questionnaire and the schedule, to tables and graphs and all things mathematical. What kind of people, and how many of them, succeed in passing for White? What are the differential rates of interaction among neighbours of similar and disparate ethnicity? These are questions the answers to which might be elegantly arranged in graphs and tables, and they are questions which it is proper to ask. But, alas, the answers made here cannot be given mathematical expression. They are most of them impressionistic. That is a pity, but it is better than nothing. Observer participation has severe limitations, but the subterfuge which inevitably surrounds passing for White renders quite impractical the use of ancillary statistically based techniques.

One further difficulty inherent in the technique of observer participation is the danger it poses with regard to the formation of obtrusive value-judgements. It is impossible to live and work with other human beings for any length of time without finding one's sympathies, willy-nilly, drawn to one side or the other. Since it is not possible altogether to avoid value-judgements, it is only fair that they should be made explicit. Let it be understood, then, that the writer finds colour prejudice, and the grotesque structure of laws that perpetuate it, abhorrent and execrable. If the reader hears axes being ground in the background he has at least been given fair warning.

NOTES

1 W. W. Waller, *The Sociology of Teaching*, New York, John Wiley, 1932.

2 C. E. Bidwell, 'The School as a Formal Organization', in J. G. March (ed.), *Handbook of Organizations*, Chicago, Rand McNally, 1965, pp. 972–1022.

3 J. Floud and A. H. Halsey, *The Sociology of Education*, Oxford, Blackwell, 1958.

4 For an introduction to the literature on South African race relations the reader can do no better than to consult Pierre van den Berghe's *South Africa: a Study in Conflict*, Middletown, Wesleyan University Press, 1965, and the select bibliography contained therein.

Sheila Patterson's *Colour and Culture in South Africa*, London, Routledge and Kegan Paul, 1953, is perhaps the best-known work on the Coloured people. Dickie-Clark's *The Marginal Situation*, London, Routledge and Kegan Paul, 1966, while more limited in scope, is unrivalled in the field. S. P. Cilliers's *The Coloured People of South Africa*, Cape Town, Banier, 1963, is a useful compendium of information, based largely on the 1960 *Census Report*.

There is no lengthy treatment of passing for White in non-fictional volumes on South Africa, but the topic is dealt with cursorily by C. Dover, *Half-Caste*, London, Secker and Warburg, 1937; *Report of the Commission of the Cape Coloured Population of the Union* (U.G. 54/1937), S. Patterson, 1953, *op. cit.*; S. G. Millin, *The People of South Africa*, New York, Knopf, 1954; E. V. S. Stonequist, *The Marginal Man*, New York, Russell and Russell, 1961; H. F. Dickie-Clark, 1966, *op. cit.* Well-known fictional works dealing specifically with the topic include S. G. Millin's *God's Stepchildren*, London, Constable, 1924, and A. Fugard's *The Blood Knot*, Cape Town, Simondium Publishers, 1964.

5 Van Rooy, quoted by B. Bunting in *The Rise of the South African Reich*, Harmondsworth, Penguin, 1964, p. 194.

6 Popular histories of education in South Africa are curiously reticent on the subject. See, for example, E. G. Malherbe, *Education in South Africa*, Cape Town, Juta, 1925; M. E. McKerron, *A History of Education in South Africa*, Pretoria, Von Schaik, 1934; E. G. Pells, *300 Years of Education in South Africa*, Cape Town, Juta, 1954.

B

Chapter One

THE PEOPLE OF COLANDER

Every school is embedded in a community and is to a greater or lesser extent transformed by it. If the social structure of Colander High School is to be understood, it must be understood in the light of the social structure of Colander, the suburb of Cape Town in which the school is situated.

Colander is bisected geographically and socially by a major thorough-fare which carries dense traffic. The area east of the road is almost entirely residential, and those who live there look down their noses upon their less fortunate neighbours to the west, living in an area devoted largely to light industry. At right angles to this thoroughfare, and crossing it, is Middle Street.

A typical Middle Street house is one of a long row of almost identical seedy-looking bungalows, built many years ago, roofed with corru-gated iron, and joined at each end to its neighbours or separated by a narrow aperture. A long white-washed wall, crumbling with neglect, and a rusty iron-grille gate bar the way from the street. The gate leads straight on to the narrow verandah, for there is no garden, or, at most, a yard or so of potted plants. The heavy green door is shut and the cur-tains of the front rooms are drawn under the fierce African sun. A long, dark corridor, with one or two bedrooms adjoining it, leads to a combined sitting- and dining-room. The doors of the bedrooms are shut, but a furtive glance reveals a bleak room containing two or three beds, several plain wooden chairs, an unpretentious wardrobe, and a dowdy Pre-Raphaelite print on the wall. Most of the space in the neat but drab sitting-cum-dining-room is taken up by a large and highly polished table, surmounted by a posy of artificial flowers. Bordering the wall are heavy Victorian armchairs, grease-stained and inconspicu-ously patched. There are no sideboards or ornaments, but on the wall are more Pre-Raphaelite prints, and some wedding photographs. In a prominent position is a florid radiogram, tuned to the commercial radio. This is the visitors' room, scarcely used: the social centre of the home is the kitchen. The rent for such a house is perhaps six to eight pounds per month west of the main thoroughfare, or eighteen to twenty pounds east of it.

Most of the other houses in Middle Street differ from this one only in detail. The nearer the industry, the older the coats of paint, and the iron-grille gate is replaced by a rickety wooden one. The nearer the mountain the more spacious the rooms; the iron-grille gate is more elaborate and there is a brightly polished brass knocker on the door; and the prints on the wall are newer, the Pre-Raphaelites giving way to Tretchikoff.

At the eastern extremity of Middle Street lies Upper Colander, so called in order that it might be differentiated from Colander; here live the 'respectable' people, the cable-joiners, warehouse clerks, lorry drivers. The Ratepayers' Association frequently receives complaints from Upper Colander householders that many sellers of property in the adjoining streets advertise their houses as being in the district.

At the western extremity of Middle Street are tumbled and rotting tenements, pregnant with the smell of sour urine, and resounding with the cries of countless urchins. The rooms are cold, bare, and tawdry, the walls mildewed. Here live the 'roffs' (roughs), the linesmen and shunters, the night-shift workers. Among the 'respectable' people they have the reputation of drunkenness, wife-beating, and sexual promiscuity. The contempt in which they are held by middle-class Whites – and their anomalous position in South Africa's colour-estate system – is illustrated by the following passage, abstracted from a textbook in current use in South African universities.

Profound degeneration has been brought about among a considerable portion of the White population. It has produced a class known as the 'poor White', numbering anything up to several hundred thousand, according to the definition given the term. It comprises all those Whites who, through weakness of character, moral fiber, or intellect, or through sheer force of uncontrollable circumstances, have dropped well below the average European standard of living. They have given up the fight to maintain their status as aristocrats. While climatic degeneration, the effects of isolation and the consequent lack of educational facilities, or disaster by diseases, flood, or drought have been potent factors in the genesis of this class, the presence of a vast non-European population at a low standard of living has produced much of the demoralization characteristic of them. There are poor in every country. But they are a comparatively virile poor, earning their bread by the sweat of their brows. The poor White is a different kind of being. He does not do 'kaffir' work; that would not be right for a member of the dominant race. There is no other work of which he is capable. So, in effect, he does little or no work of any sort.[1]

Colander, then, is, as far as middle-class White Capetonians are concerned, a run-down working-class area, but within its limits there are clearly recognizable degrees of 'respectability'.[2]

It has for many years had the reputation of attracting the 'better class' of Coloured people, and the 'poorer class' of Whites. If we except those Whites with the highest status (those living in Upper Colander and those Coloureds with the lowest status (those living in the westernmost areas), the reputation is well founded. This is accepted by Colander residents themselves. Even the Whites admit that 'Europeans don't come to Colander unless they can't afford to go somewhere else', and 'the Coloured folk are of the better class here and people can see it every day'. Thus there are many Whites who live in humble areas of Colander, and many Coloureds who live in prestigious areas; and there are many Coloureds who live in tidier, cleaner houses than their White neighbours, and who pursue occupations more prestigious than those of most Whites. It would seem that such a situation would lead to considerable hostility between White and Coloured, in view of the number of commentators who have reported that in societies stratified along colour lines it is the poorest of the Whites who are characterized by the most hostile prejudices against non-White co-members of their society.[3] This study can only support Bettelheim and Janowitz's conclusion that it is not possible to postulate simple and direct relations between social class and prejudice.[4] A relationship of 'live and let live' seems only sensible in a community in which few are unequivocally White. 'Everybody has some blood; so nobody can bother,' they say. And, 'We have to live together, so you can't go around denouncing your neighbours.'

The people of Colander tend to think of themselves not so much in terms of colour categories but as 'respectable' people and 'roff' people, categories that cut across colour lines. In attempting to establish racial categories in a more clear-cut way, the government is acting against tradition, for, as if in recognition of their close cultural and racial affinity to the Whites, the Coloured people of South Africa have always enjoyed a 'special relationship' with the Whites: in the Cape of Good Hope Coloureds were in full possession of the franchise, sharing all political rights with Whites; and they did not lose these rights until the South Africa Act was amended in 1956, against sustained opposition. Unlike the *Bantu* people they are regarded as permanent residents in the White towns, are not subject to extremely restricted residential rights, a degrading system of influx control, and the registration of service contracts. Unlike the Bantu people, they retain a foothold in the skilled trades and have a limited right to strike. Relations between White and Coloured have been particularly cordial in Cape Town, where the City Council initially refused to co-operate with the government in the de-marcation of *Group Areas*, preferring to leave matters undisturbed. White and Coloured still, in 1960, shared the municipal franchise on a common roll, and in 1963 there were seven non-Whites on the Council. But even in Cape Town Colander has been a special case.

Not only were Coloureds, until recently, given full political rights; intermarriage between Whites and Coloureds was tolerated, especially in Colander, where there was a great deal of intermarriage between the races during the two world wars.[5] The Scots and, before them, the Germans are said to have been the men who most often married across the colour line. Many of the Germans were peasants and liked Coloured wives because they had the reputation of being hard-working. Such intermarriage appears to have been accepted with equanimity, and even now in Colander the Whites tend to shrug off such matters with the comment, 'Everyone wants to better themselves – you can under-stand that.' Quite foreign to them is the sanctimonious disapproval sometimes voiced in the columns of the Capetonian press. 'It's just a simple old home-truth of human affairs,' writes a columnist in the *Cape Times* (addressing himself, by implication, to Coloureds). 'It applies to all peoples and has applied at all times in all countries that if you try to be what you are not you are heading for heartbreak; if you accept what you are and face the world with self-respect for what you are, you can make a world much more to your liking.'

Despite the vast edifice of discriminating legislation which the government has erected, there is still a sense of common identity between the Whites and Coloureds of Colander which both groups are anxious to preserve. Recently, there have been manifestations of hostility between the two groups, and several cases of apparently wan-ton assault by Whites upon Coloureds have come to light. Afrikaans-speaking railway workers, recently settled in the suburb, are the chief culprits: they call their neighbours 'daa'ie Hotnots' (them Hottentots). And just as Whites sometimes despise their Coloured neighbours so do Coloureds sometimes despise their White neighbours: 'Afrikaners are thick-soled and thick-skinned country bumpkins'; 'an Afrikaner will exploit you, an Englishman abuse you, but a Jew will invest in you'. The variants of the theme of colour prejudice are endless. However, these expressions of hostility are seen by Colander as a regrettable change from a more idyllic state of affairs.

The precise quality of this change is difficult to gauge. Informants naturally differ in their assessment of its extent, for they have had different experiences. All, however, hark back to the Golden Age when relations between Colander Whites and Coloureds were 'excellent' or 'very good' and when 'things worked themselves out'. There are many who say that they were 'not aware of the race' of their neighbours, and that they had many friends of both races. Upon closer inquiry their replies suggest, however, that the only Coloured neighbours with whom Whites would consort with any degree of intimacy were those who were 'just like Whites', and that Coloured persons who had succeeded in striking up a close friendship with Whites were fair of complexion. A 'respectable Coloured' was sometimes referred to as 'one that mixes in with Whites', or as a 'Coloured European'. Manifestly Coloured persons attending White churches generally sat inconspicuously at the back. Even in the thirties, people of Colander say, fair-skinned sons would not introduce a dark-skinned mother to their White friends 'until they knew you didn't mind', and when they did introduce such a mother they did so anxiously, 'like a university graduate introducing a grandfather who was only a labourer'. It is possible that the rosy picture which people of Colander paint of times past is a reflection less of the truth than of the desire which they have to maintain friendly relations between Whites and Coloureds, despite external pressures. The Golden Age is thus, in Malinowskian terms, the social charter for the continuance of what, in South Africa, is now an extraordinary relationship.

What accounts for the extraordinary nature of this relationship? The suggestion advanced here is that affinities of socio-economic status confuse the colour line in Colander and stimulate the association of Coloureds of high socio-economic status relative to other Coloureds with Whites of low socio-economic status relative to other Whites.

A survey of the occupations of the parents of Colander High School children (see Appendix A) can probably be taken as typical of White Colander. A small proportion of the parents fall into categories typical of poor Whites (e.g. railway worker, bus conductor) or typical of Coloureds (e.g. housemaid, postman, clothing machinist, fisherman), but a very much larger proportion of occupations reported are skilled or semi-skilled manual occupations. Among the actively employed, 67·4 per cent of the fathers and 73·9 per cent of the mothers are engaged in such occupations. The point to be noted is that the occupational statuses and incomes of Whites and Coloureds in Colander are more nearly comparable than are those of the total populations of Whites and Coloureds in both the Republic and the Cape Peninsula. In the Cape Peninsula as a whole, 64·5 per cent of the economically active Coloured males are craftsmen or production workers,[7] but only 28·9 per cent of economically active White males have these occupations. Among the Colander High fathers, 67·4 per cent fall into the similar category of skilled and semi-skilled workers. In other words, although Colander High is a White school, a large majority of the fathers are in occupations comparable to those pursued by most Coloured men in the Cape Peninsula. The gap between the median incomes of White and Coloured males in South Africa is smallest among transport workers (R 1067 or £533.5), clerical workers (R 1143) and service workers (R 1199).[8] And it is to these latter occupations that a considerable proportion of the fathers of Colander High pupils belong. Many of these fathers are artisans, and where artisans belong to a trade union both White and Coloured receive the same pay. The Whites of Colander, then, belong to the *working class*, and their socio-economic status is roughly the equivalent of that of their 'better-class' Coloured neighbours.

The composition of the households and the pattern of neighbouring of the Colander High parents are typical not only of the working class in other parts of the world but are similar to the pattern of life of the Coloured people of Colander. The composition of the households to which the pupils of Colander High belong appears to follow a pattern resembling that associated with working-class status in sociological literature.[9] Analysis of responses to a questionnaire[10] administered to the pupils of Colander High indicates that the composition of the households to which the children belong is notable for two characteristics: the high proportion (23·4 per cent) in which the father is reported not present, and the high incidence (34·8 per cent) reported as containing relatives other than members of the nuclear family. In this last respect they resemble 'upper-class' Coloured households.[11]

Patterns of neighbouring in Colander are altogether different from those found in Cape Town's more prestigious suburbs, where primly kept hedges are symbolic of a desire to keep oneself to oneself. In Colander neighbours, both White and Coloured, are ever in and out of one another's houses, especially 'in time of trouble'; and their children play together rumbustiously in the street outside. Children delight in writing essays about their neighbours, and the kind of neighbours they like are cheerful and co-operative: 'If we are in any kind of trouble and we ask for any help they are very obliging.' The kind they dislike are those who 'walk around the house with long faces and don't even come out', or who fail to adjust themselves to communal living: 'When the dog starts barking they run out like a lot of scarecrows as if something terrible has happened.'

Afrikaans is the language of the majority of the Coloured people,[12] and, in answer to the questionnaire, children attending Colander High reported that 11·7 per cent of their households contained one or more persons (excluding boarders) who spoke more Afrikaans than English at home.[13] That figure probably constitutes a conservative estimate of the amount of Afrikaans actually spoken in the homes – just under half of the forty-odd families I visited contained one or more persons who admitted to being 'Afrikaans-speaking'. This estimate, too, might be deceptively low, for I formed the firm impression that the use of Afrikaans at home was regarded as a matter of shame, and there was certainly a great reluctance to admit to it. More than once I heard a mother insist indignantly, in a strong Afrikaans accent, that 'We don't speak the language in this house!' One even blamed her self-styled 'thick accent' (strongly Afrikaans) on her new dentures. On several occasions when I attempted to pursue a conversation in Afrikaans the atmosphere turned icy, and frantic attempts were made to resume the conversation in English. This is an uncommon reaction in Afrikaans-speaking homes outside the area, or in manifestly Coloured homes within it, the members of which, in my experience, commonly express delight that a 'rooinek' (a Briton) should essay the language. Part of the reluctance to admit to Afrikaans as a home language is due to the fact that Afrikaans is the language, by and large, of the 'roffs' who live west of the road: Afrikaners are castigated in school essays as 'uncouth', 'noisy', and 'quarrelsome'.

We have seen that in Colander there is considerable similarity in economic status and in way of life between the Whites and the Coloureds. A study of attitudes in Colander suggests not only that similarity of socio-economic status makes for harmonious relations between races, but also that, contrary to racial ideologies, people are more inclined to categorize other people on the basis of economic status and way of life than on the basis of race and colour. It is true that in Colander class and colour often coincide. The 'respectable' people live to the east of the main thoroughfare, the 'roffs' west of it; and it is the Coloureds who inhabit the most densely populated and shabby areas west of the main road, and the Whites who live in the newer, more prosperous-looking parts. But despite this, the line which the people of Colander draw between White and Coloured is not an incisive one. Residents of long standing in Colander do not follow the common South African practice of lumping together all Whites on the one hand and all non-Whites on the other; rather do they lump 'Europeans' and Coloureds together, and differentiate them from 'the native'. Within the White/Coloured group a distinction is drawn between 'Malays' and the nominally Christian; within the White/ Coloured Christian group a sharp distinction is drawn between the 'respectable' people and the 'roffs'. The words of a White Colander housewife illustrate this:

> We used to live in Walmer Estate [1930s] but the Malays came and so we all moved out because if you stay there you get classed with them. There were very good families there, but we all went. But people should mix if they want and don't if they don't want to. It's a social thing. Why must they make a law? If a native bought that house next door then of course I would object, but Coloured families are respectable. After a bit you become intimate and you see what they're like. It all depends on what people are like. White skollies [petty criminals] are as bad as Coloured skollies. And these farmer types [Afrikaners] know nothing and they come here with their mouth open. They don't like to see a Coloured family with a home as nice as a European. Give them enough rope and they'll hang themselves. Verwoerd is skrik [afraid]. He doesn't want to do anything much for the working European or the Coloured people but the natives will get anything they want because Verwoerd is skrik.

The distinction made between the 'respectable' and the 'roff' blur the colour line, for it is a distinction based on social class rather than on complexion. 'We don't go around here for the people are not worth mixing with,' complained the mother of one of my pupils at Colander High. 'There used to be Coloureds living here in this street – tip-top Coloureds – but they had to move because the area has been declared a White zone: and then rubbishy Whites move in, and they make it so obvious.' There is some similarity in this regard between Colander and Bahia, where 'A poor White man is a Negro and a rich Negro a White man.'[14]

It is not only the close affinity of social and economic status in itself that gives to Whites and Coloureds a sense of common identity, but also the fact that the economic conditions of all residents of Colander separate them from other groups. It has already been pointed out that the Whites of Colander are poorer than the majority of South African Whites, but they are not simply at the bottom of the ladder – they are beyond the pale. The social-class hierarchy of White South Africans has not yet been the object of substantial study, but few observers would seriously quarrel with Andreski's estimation that 'Personal contacts between Whites are marked by easy informality, expressions of deference never assume extreme forms, differences in manners are relatively slight, and even among English-speaking people "stand-offishness" is incomparably less common than in England,' and that 'In comparison with Europe outside Scandinavia, the most salient feature of this stratification is the relative attenuation of what is called social distance, in spite of great difference in wealth.'[15] However, members of the very lowest reaches of the White South African social-class hierachy are not included in this description; such people as White residents of Colander are the object of their compatriots' ridicule: 'If you want to make somebody laugh,' said a Colander High School teacher, 'say Colander.' There is, in fact, a tendency amongst Capetonians to think of all residents of Colander, including Whites, as Coloured. The logic of the Capetonian's thinking is simple. There are White South Africans who are very poor, but their number is so insignificant that they have been endowed with the peculiar appellation of 'Poor Whites' and are described in newspaper editorials as a 'problem'. That their number is now small is largely a result of apartheid: most unskilled workers in the Republic are non-White, because occupations which require skills above a certain level are, in general, reserved for Whites through the Industrial Conciliation Act of 1924 (and subsequent amendments). There are virtually no White domestic servants, no White road navvies, no White dock labourers. It becomes easy to equate light skin complexion with the possession of occupational skills and a relatively high standard of living. And from that point it is but a short step to the belief that relatively unskilled White workers are 'not really White, dear'. 'Poor Whites' are poor, by this reasoning, not because they are unskilled, but because they are not altogether White. So, poverty, relatively unskilled manual occupation, and residence in a run-down suburb are equated not with lower-middle-class White status but with 'Coloured blood': *class* is perceived as a correlate of *estate*. As a defence against this prejudice residents of Colander often heatedly deny to other Whites that they live in Colander and mendaciously profess to residence in nearby suburbs.

In the Capetonian's mind poverty is associated with 'Coloured blood'. So, to some extent, is the Afrikaans language, for Afrikaans is the home language of the majority of the Coloured people. So, where a swarthy skin leaves the Capetonian in doubt as to a person's colour – and few Whites in Colander possess a skin so fair as to inhibit all speculation as to their race – and where that swarthy skin is also associated with poverty, then his doubts tend to be resolved one way or the other according to the person's home language. Thus the Capetonian's tendency to think of the White people of Colander as Coloured is given added impetus by the fact that many residents of Colander speak Afrikaans, or a mixture of English and Afrikaans, at home. And the Capetonian's suspicion that the Whites of Colander are really Coloured because many of them are Afrikaans-speaking, is further strengthened by the fact that Colander is a mixed residential area in which avowed Coloured persons live in close proximity to White persons. All this encourages the Whites of Colander to think of themselves not so much as members of an exclusive White group but as members of a Coloured/White group. For a White person is only as White as he is thought to be.

Residents of Colander not only feel themselves different from the superordinate White group; they are also concerned to preserve the distinction between themselves and the 'lower' racial groups.

There is a 'we-feeling' between the Whites and Coloureds of Colander, a sense of common identity. Colour prejudice is not absent among either Whites or Coloureds but it tends to be directed against Bantu rather than against Coloureds. This prejudice affords both Whites and Coloureds a comfortable feeling of superiority and a closer identification with the superordinate White estate. But prejudice is not directed solely against the Bantu, and it is instructive to identify its targets. Before and during the 1939–45 war many Jews settled in Colander and lived in rooms above their business premises. Almost all of them have now left the area to live in more 'respectable' suburbs. They recall how they were the object of street-corner taunts in Colander (e.g. 'I had a piece of pork and I put it on a fork . . .') and some of them attribute this hostility to their avowed feeling of superiority to the majority of those who live in Colander. Afrikaans-speaking newcomers to the area, mostly poor and highly colour-conscious railway workers, are widely reviled as 'farmer types' for their cavalier treatment of 'respectable' Coloureds. White and Coloured alike recount with every sign of horror the incident in which a Coloured school headmaster was beaten up on his Colander doorstep, without apparent motive, by White Afrikaans-speaking neighbours. The most recent wave of immigrants to Colander – Portuguese, Greeks, Italians – have taken over the economic role once played by Jews and have become the focus of much ill-feeling: 'The Portuguese – you know, with the fish carts and things – they can come in but our respectable Coloured people has got to get out.' Pass-White children, resident in Colander, who attempt to enrol in a White high school outside the area, may be accused of 'disloyalty', especially by older White residents, and some have, for this very reason, been refused admission to Colander High when they subsequently applied for it. Anti-Muslim prejudice is common to perhaps all those who live in Colander (except Muslims) but is found in its most virulent form among Coloureds, where a 'Malay' stereotype is well established. According to the stereotype 'Malays' practise nepotism, are 'close', proud, do not attempt to pass for White,[16] and are guilty of 'toenaadering' – of tamely co-operating with the government in the implementation of its policy of racial segregation. Thus, hostility is directed not only against Bantu but also against all those, irrespective of their colour, who threaten to disrupt the sense of identity shared by the Whites and Coloureds of Colander.

Thus the socio-economic and cultural affinity between Colander Whites and Coloureds, together with the White Capetonian's tendency to regard Colander Whites as 'really' Coloured, generates a we-feeling between the two groups in Colander and permits the emergence of cross-cutting loyalties based on socio-economic status rather than colour.

On only one occasion – during a recent period of crisis – have I observed the we-feeling partially disintegrating and the Whites, through community agencies, discriminating in favour of 'roff' Whites and against 'roff' Coloureds. The Western Province Land Tenure Advisory Board sat to consider zoning various regions of Colander under the Group Areas Act. The School Committee of Colander High School joined in an astonishing alliance with the Nationalist Party and the Dutch Reformed Church in advocating that a slum area, inhabited predominantly by 'roff' Coloureds, should be zoned for exclusive White occupation. The Chairman of the School Committee explained: 'If it was declared Coloured the White [and near-White] people would be declared Coloured [under the Population Registration Act] or else would have to get out. In any case there were so many Coloureds there only because of speculator landlords who sub-let a dwelling to three or four families to ensure regular payment of rent.'

NOTES

1 E. G. Pells, *300 Years of Education in South Africa*, Cape Town, Juta, 1957, p. 7.

2 The investigation of social stratification within the White group in South Africa has not yet been the object of extensive or profound inquiry. If I employ the terms 'working class' and 'middle class' (although I suspect that 'status groups' would be more appropriate) I do so because they are in common parlance and are elastic in connotation. Some White residents of Colander themselves use the terms.

3 For example, G. Myrdal, *An American Dilemma*, New York, Harper and Bros., 1944, pp. 597–8; G. W. Allport, *The Nature of Prejudice*, New York, Doubleday and Co., 1958, p. 78. S. Andreski comments on the South African scene in *The Uses of Comparative Sociology*, Berkeley, University of California Press, 1964, pp. 264–5.

4 B. Bettelheim and J. Janowitz, *Social Change and Prejudice*, New York, The Free Press, 1950, pp. 20–3.

5 For an historical precedent for the social mixing of some Whites and Coloureds see W. P. Carstens, *The Social Structure of a Cape Coloured Reserve*, London, Oxford University Press, 1966.

6 The socio-economic classification of occupations used here is one adapted to local conditions by E. Batson (see Appendix A).

7 *Population Census, 1960, Sample Tabulation No. 4: Incomes.*

8 *Population Census, 1960, Sample Tabulation No. 4: Incomes.* In 1960 R 1 was worth £0·5 or U.S. $1.40.

9 See, for example, M. Kerr, *The People of Ship Street*, London, Routledge and Kegan Paul, 1958; and M. Young and P. Willmott, *Family and Kinship in East London*, London, Routledge and Kegan Paul, 1957.

10 One cannot go around Colander asking people questions about their relatives or they will suspect one of attempting to discover pass-Whites in their midst. The only alternative means of eliciting quantifiable information about household composition – the administration of a questionnaire to the pupils of Colander High – was accepted with misgivings, for it was thought that young children, many of whom are below average intelligence, would find difficulty in giving reliable answers, and that this difficulty would not be lessened by the fact that no pilot questionnaire was to be administered. The furore among parents when they discovered that 'personal questions' had been asked of their children amply justified the decision not to administer a pilot. The misgivings concerning the children's ability to cope with the questionnaire were likewise justified when only 141 of the 174 responses were accepted as reasonably reliable. Of the 26 responses obtained from the youngest and least intelligent class, only 14 were accepted. The oldest and brightest class experienced less difficulty in answering the questions accurately, and 29 of their 32 responses were accepted and included in the final calculations. Those which were dismissed as possibly not reliable were those in which responses did not tally with the certain knowledge of some households which I and other teachers had, or which did not tally with answers given by siblings or with answers given to other questions inserted into the questionnaire as a cross-check. The questionnaire is reproduced as Appendix B.

11 S. P. Cilliers, *The Coloureds of South Africa*, Cape Town, Banier, 1963, p. 25.

12 88·6 per cent have Afrikaans as their home language, 10·2 per cent English, 0·9 per cent have both, and 0·3 per cent another. See *Census Report, 1960, Sample Tabulation No. 2*.

13 Twenty out of 171 households. Of these, 9 contained more than one person who was reported as speaking more Afrikaans than English. Two other households contained one person who spoke more Italian than English.

14 D. Pierson, *Negroes in Brazil*, Chicago, University of Chicago Press, 1942, p. 348.

15 S. Andreski, *op. cit.*, p. 270.

16 S. Patterson, in *Colour and Culture in South Africa*, London, Routledge and Kegan Paul, 1953, p. 319, claims that 'Malays do not feel themselves inferior because they are not White, nor do they copy European ways nor attempt to "pass" into the European group', a claim echoed by L. Marquard in *The Peoples and Policies of South Africa*, London, Oxford University Press, 1962, p. 85. This is not altogether justified for I know some 'Malays' who have surreptitiously enrolled in White schools and universities.

Chapter Two

SOCIAL MOBILITY AMONG THE CAPE COLOURED

The we-feeling shared by the Whites and Coloureds of Colander, examined in the previous chapter, makes the suburb a well-nigh ideal environment in which to practise passing for White. Passing is in fact endemic to the suburb – hence the epithet 'Colander White' – and to Colander High School. In order to elucidate the consequences which this has for the school, we must first examine the process of passing for White *per se*.

In this chapter an account is given of social mobility among the Cape Coloured people, and the suggestion is advanced that this mobility cannot be fully comprehended except in the context of Coloured/White relations. Upward mobility among the Coloured people and among the White people is, for those Coloureds whose compexion is fair and who therefore have the potential to pass for White, one continuous process.

Commentators discuss the Coloured people in terms of three 'classes'. Neither the designation of the units nor their number appears convincing to Coloured informants. Van der Merwe[1] admits that 'No clearly demarcated class grouping exists in the minds of the Coloured [Stellenbosch] community', but nevertheless, for the purposes of rating, names three 'classes'. Patterson,[2] Cilliers,[3] van den Berghe,[4] and the Cape Coloured Commission[5] likewise speak in terms of 'upper', 'middle', and 'lower classes'. But discussions with some two dozen Colander Coloureds, mostly teachers and artisans, indicate that Coloured Capetonians, other than those who profess Marxism, do not themselves think in terms of 'classes', nor does the number three figure in their thinking: they think in terms of a continuum along which are marked various points representing achievements in the process of upward social mobility, rather like the squares in a game of snakes and ladders; and the points are six in number.

At the first and most lowly point is the farm labourer, despised by residents of Colander as a country bumpkin: 'He's raw and he doesn't know that there are places where a Coloured person is not dragged out of bed at five in the morning but is treated like a human being. In town we have regulation hours.'

He reaches the second point on the continuum when he moves to town. Rural-urban migration has proceeded at a rapid pace[6] and is invariably described by informants as part and parcel of the continuum and not as a qualitatively different process. Presuming the migrant is not fortunate enough to have relatives who have already a bridgehead in the city, claim informants, he lives at first in a 'pondok', or corrugated-iron shanty, like those that were once common in the shanty-towns, such as the old Windermere, in the Cape Town area. He is described by informants as likely to be illiterate, generally unemployed, and to burden the welfare agencies during the winter months. If he is unsuccessful in his attempts to acquire employment, he may lose all incentive to work and spend his time drinking, gambling, and indulging in petty crime. Such as he are commonly referred to as 'skollies'.

Although today it is common to hear any kind of delinquent referred to as a 'skollie', a clear distinction should be made between the part-time 'holhanger' who has a job most of the time but who spends his evenings hanging about on street corners and who may indulge in a little petty crime of the sort practised by White 'ducktails', and those for whom street-corner life and petty crime are a vocation rather than a hobby. This distinction is no longer generally made, but it is to the latter group that the term 'skollie' is more correctly applied. The 'skollie' is not simply a delinquent: his group is partly self-perpetuating, 'skollies' often being the children of 'skollies'. In the days when liquor for non-Whites was still rationed to two bottles a day, they earned their living 'mailing' for 'smoggelhuise' (shebeens), and also by dagga (hemp) peddling, petty theft, and robbery. 'Skollies' have developed a social organization and a way of life which sets them apart from the majority of Coloured people. This fact is of importance if only because its existence unduly colours the Whites' conception of the Coloured community. The dichotomy which many White persons make between 'respectable' Coloureds and 'skollies' – which carries the imputation that 'skollies' constitute a considerable proportion of the Coloured community – is indicative of nothing so much as the Whites' ignorance of their Coloured compatriots.

If the aspirant to upward social mobility does not fall by the wayside among the 'skollies' and is lucky enough to land a good job for perhaps three or four pounds a week, claim informants, he moves up to the next point on the continuum. He builds himself a semi-permanent structure, built to last about five years, such as those which are to be found along Settlers' Way, on the Cape Flats, and at Retreat, and perhaps invites some of his country relatives to share it with him.

The next step is more difficult. If he acquires a sufficient degree of urban sophistication and accumulates a moderate amount of capital, according to informants, he moves to a sub-economic housing estate, such as those known as Silvertown, Bridgetown, Steenberg, and Bonteheuvel (described contemptuously by intellectuals as 'locations'), or to District Six, the Malay Quarter, or to some of the more unsavoury parts of lower Woodstock and Salt River. With this step he joins the ranks of the majority of his fellows, the people who have spent perhaps six years at school, the people who form coon troupes (execrated by the intellectuals for their Uncle Tom image), the people who live in houses with names like 'Utopia', 'Greenfields', or 'Hightrees', and who share them with two or three other households.

Informants claim that access to the next point on the continuum, occupied by the group of artisans, skilled and semi-skilled workers (such as those who predominate in Crawford, the older parts of Athlone, Woodstock, and Salt River), depends on the acquisition of occupational skills and the husbanding of economic resources. The training required for entry into a trade is, for many, prohibitively expensive, and their upward progress is thereby brought to a halt. Economic failure, precipitated perhaps by too large a family, means slipping down the scale again. Economic success provides an opportunity for moving up into the ranks of the élite. Parents of this group will attempt to ease their children's upward mobility by encouraging them to enter a trade, a white-collar occupation, or, best of all, the teaching profession.

So far no gates have been firmly closed against the aspirant to upward social mobility within the Coloured group: all depends on industry and thrift. 'It's like this,' explained one man who had made the grade, 'when you get a job you are a Have-Got and your neighbours are Have-Not-Gots. So you look around, and say: "Where are the birds of my feather?" You find them and move in. Then you make more money, and soon your neighbours are once again Have-Not-Gots. So once again you look around for birds of your own feather. And so it goes on.' But the next step, entry into the élite, is more formidable, and success depends on factors some of which are ascribed rather than achieved.

The élite consists of businessmen and professional people, the people whom Patterson and van der Merwe describe as 'upper middle class'.[7] To become a successful businessman requires capital, and few are able to amass it. To enter a profession requires a lengthy education, and few are able to afford it. And neither wealth nor education alone, say informants, is sufficient qualification for entry into the élite. In the first place, the successful candidate must have a 'respectable' way of life, for the norm of 'respectability' is every bit as important among the Coloured people as it is among 'lower-middle-class Whites'.[8] He must live in a fashionable area such as Walmer Estate (Woodstock), Sunlands Estate (Lansdowne), Claremont (between the railway line and Third Avenue), and Wynberg (Park Road area). It is a help if he comes from a 'good family' and if he speaks English. It is extremely helpful if he comes from a 'good' Coloured school, such as Trafalgar High, Livingstone High, Cressy – or any White school. Entry into the élite is eased considerably by the possession of a fair complexion and European features. Indicative of the esteem in which these features are held by Coloured people are concoctions advertised in *Drum* and *Golden City Post* (which cater for a largely non-White readership) which purport to lighten the complexion ('A man's skin gets lighter, brighter') or straighten the hair ('You too can have straight and beautiful hair'). However, as van der Merwe[9] points out, a dark skin will not necessarily prevent a man from acquiring élite status.

Those who rank immediately below the élite may be presented with the choice of either moving up into the élite or of leapfrogging over it into the lower ranks of the White estate – a process that is known as *passing for White*. The year 1857, in which the Groote Kerk of the Dutch Reformed Church in Cape Town became 'all White' for the first time, can be taken as a landmark at which passing, as analytically distinct from miscegenation, became of significance. The pace at which the process has proceeded from time to time cannot be precisely estimated. It is probable that it has quickened in recent years, for the rapid absorption of Coloureds into industry in the 1930s, and the subsequent rise in the Coloured standard of living, has made passing increasingly feasible from a financial point of view. Moreover, the incentive to pass has increased as a result of recent legislation which has added to the innumerable humiliations of apartheid, made the acquisition of various relatively well-paid occupations difficult for Coloured persons to enter,[10] and threatened to bring the entire process to a halt. The extent to which passing has occurred, as even the Cape Coloured Commission[11] confesses, cannot be calculated with any precision, for, naturally, those who have succeeded in passing take every precaution to prevent their White compatriots from discovering this fact. It is probable that most of those who have the ability to pass do so, for few Coloureds of fair complexion live in manifestly Coloured areas such as District Six; and common observation makes it clear that many more so-called 'doubtful cases' are to be found in the White than in the Coloured group. A popular South African writer elegantly defines a Coloured person as 'one who has failed to pass as a White'.[12]

The process of passing for White is made feasible, in the first place, by the fact that the cultures of the White and Coloured peoples are very similar, though there are differences. Some of the differences, such as the Mohammedan religion of the minority, are obvious. Also obvious is the use of Afrikaans as a home language. The pass-White will often adopt English as his first language, but if he does not he will at least expunge from his vocabulary words and phrases which can be identified as belonging specifically to the Coloured argot. Equally obvious is the relative poverty of the Coloured people, and with it, the rumbustious way of life which seems to be associated with low-status groups the world over. This the aspirant must relinquish. There are also various other differences, such as loyalty to a coon troupe, or a taste for dagga, which must be concealed. The subtler differences, a desire for certain foods, perhaps, or a pronounced anti-Muslim prejudice, are not so readily recognized by White persons as primarily Coloured traits and, for this reason, aspirants are more careless about owning to them.

Passing for White is made feasible, in the second place, by the fact that there are infinite gradations between White and non-White skins and physiognomies, so that it is often not possible to tell from physical features alone to which race a particular person belongs. These infinite gradations owe their existence to the extensive miscegenation which began with the earliest Dutch settlement in South Africa and which has continued ever since.[13] Jeffrys[14] argues convincingly that since by the end of the seventeenth century there were fewer than four hundred White colonists at the Cape, and that 15–30 per cent of all marriages at the time were 'mixed', 'It is fairly safe to say that where any family has been in the country for more than two hundred years, the chance of having no infusion of colour is rather remote.' Van den Berghe[15] argues that 'One can safely estimate that anywhere from one-tenth to one-quarter of the persons classified as "White" in the Cape Province are of mixed descent, and that every "old family" from White Cape Society has genealogical connections with Coloured families.' Findlay[16] estimated in 1936 that at least 733,000 persons of 'mixed blood' were included in the 1·9 million persons then recorded as Whites in South Africa.

The difficulties experienced by those whose task it is to classify South Africans in terms of racial categories under the Population Registration Act No. 30 of 1950 (which provides for the issue of identity cards on which is recorded the race of the bearer) are as nothing compared to the embarrassment and tragedy which can be the lot of those classified. A Member of Parliament[17] cites the case of a married couple who had their race classification altered five times. They were declared Coloured in 1953; in 1955 they were accepted as White. In 1957 they were reclassified as Coloured; in 1958 as White; in 1959 as Coloured; subsequently as White. Muriel Horrell recounts many similar cases.[18] The following case study, collected by the author in Colander and the only one of its kind ever published, exposes the arbitrary nature of racial classification by demonstrating how different members of the same family can be classified disparately for the purposes of legislation and how each member may act over time and in varying circumstances as a member of more than one race.[19]

Ego's paternal great-grandfather (1) (see *Figure*, p. 21) was born in Scotland and emigrated to Stellenbosch, where he worked on the railways in an unknown capacity. He married a White woman, whom he later divorced. He then remarried, this time to a Coloured woman. They produced a son who remained in Stellenbosch as a produce farmer. He lived and worked as a White, and was married to a girl from St. Helena, about whose parents nothing is known.

They had nine children, seven sons and two daughters. Two of their sons, (2) and (3), remained in Stellenbosch. One was a produce farmer and the other owned a store. Both lived and worked as Whites, and married women who also lived and worked as Whites. The two men died before the era of race classification. Their widows survive, but it is not known if and how they have been classified. One couple was barren, and nothing is known about the children of the other.

One son, (4), moved to Colander, where he worked as an engine driver. He lived and worked as a White, but died before being classified. He married a woman who lived as White; her classification is not known. Neither their son, a teacher, nor their daughter, a cutter in the clothing industry, is married. Both live, work, and are classified as Coloured.

Another son of Ego's paternal grandfather, (5), moved to a small farm at Phillipi, and from there to Crawford, and then to Sunnyside. This area was declared Coloured under the Group Areas Act, so he moved to Lansdowne, for both he and his wife lived, worked, and were classified as White. Their unmarried daughter lives, works, and is classified as White, and is a typist.

Their married daughter, a shop assistant, and her husband, a tramway mechanic, are in the same position.

Another son of Ego's paternal grandfather, (6), moved to Lansdowne where he lived and worked as a Coloured teacher. He died before race classification. His wife lived as Coloured, but her classification is unknown. Their son became a carpenter, and their three daughters each married teachers. All these children and their spouses live, work, and are classified as Coloured. Yet another son of Ego's paternal grandfather, (7), lives with his brother in Vasco. He lives as a Coloured, but his classification is not known. He is the darkest of the family, and is not allowed to answer the door or to sit at the table when visitors are present.

One of Ego's paternal aunts, (8), lived as White and married a man who also lived as White and who had a private income. Both died before classification. They lived in Parow and had no children.

The other paternal aunt, (9), moved with her husband, who had an unspecified job in the navy, to Parow, where both lived and worked as White. She was classified White – but her husband died prior to classification. Their only son, who is in the army, lives, works, and is classified as White.

Nothing is known of Ego's maternal great-grandfather except that he was Dutch and that both he and his wife severed connection with Ego's mother when she married a Coloured man. Ego's maternal grandfather, (10), a tobacco farmer from Stellenbosch, married a woman who, like himself, lived and worked as White. Both died before classification.

They had two children. Nothing is known about the son, (11), except that he lives as White and that he severed connection with his sister, Ego's mother, (12), when she married a Coloured. She married the remaining son of Ego's paternal grandparents, (13), and moved from Stellenbosch to Maitland; thence to Tiger Valley and Crawford. Her husband was a carpenter. Both live and work as Coloured, yet both are classified as White; they find this amusing.

They had seven children, six daughters and a son. The son, (14), a clerk, lives as a Coloured, works as a White, and is not yet classified. His wife is in a similar predicament. One daughter, (15), married a shop manager. Both live and work and are classified as White. The two other married daughters, (16) and (17), one of whom is a clerk, live, work, and are classified as Coloured. Their husbands – a clerk and a carpenter – are in the same position. Ego, (18), is unmarried and lives and works as White, but had delayed applying for her Population Registration Card for fear that she might be classified Coloured. She has once been dismissed employment because she refused to produce her unemployment registration card: she previously worked as Coloured and this is stated on the card. Her two unmarried sisters, (19) and (20), a shop assistant and a nurse, both live as Coloureds, but work as White, and are classified as White.

Thus, of Ego and her siblings, two live, work, and are classified as Coloured; one lives as Coloured, works as White, but remains unclassified; two live as

Coloured but work and are classified as White; one lives and works as
White but is unclassified; and one lives and works and is classified as White:
their parents live and work as Coloureds but are classified as White. Thus do
the architects of apartheid separate the races.

Most of those who pass belong, claim informants, to the artisan
and skilled worker group. It seems probable that those who rank above
this group in the internal status hierarchy are tempted to remain within
the Coloured camp, sometimes out of political loyalty to their compatriots, and sometimes perhaps for fear of increased economic competition within the White group. Those who rank below the artisan
group seldom possess the characteristics necessary for successful passing.
The most important of these characteristics is, of course, a fair skin,
and this is found mainly among the élite and artisan group.[20] But a
fair skin is not the only qualification necessary for successful passing.
Cultural criteria must also be taken into account. And here again it is
the élite and artisan groups who possess the most qualifications for
passing. It is they who are able to afford the education necessary to
enter White occupations, the relatively high rent payable on properties
bordering White homes, the standard of living and articles of dress
which most Whites enjoy. It is they who most commonly speak English
as their first language, or who have stayed at school long enough to
acquire proficiency in it as a second language.

To facilitate the process of passing, Coloureds will, it is commonly
said, often move from the town or province where they are known.[21]
One hears of Coloureds who have moved from Johannesburg to Cape
Town for this purpose, and of others who have moved from Cape
Town to Johannesburg.[22] Dr Wollheim estimates that there are at
least 25,000 pass-Whites in Johannesburg today.[23] Many others migrate
to England, Canada, and elsewhere. But the strongest movement is
probably from the districts of the South-Western Cape – the area
which is bounded by Swellendam on the west and Uitenhage on the
east, and which includes George, Knysna, Mossel Bay, and Oudtshoorn
– to Cape Town itself. The South-Western Cape was traditionally a
farming area and the movement to town is in part a consequence of
increasing mechanization on the farms. It is also an area of traditional
intermarriage across the colour line. The Afrikaans names Van Rens-
burg, Groenewald, Jacobs, Marais, Oktober, Veldsman, Booysens,
and others, occur frequently among Coloured families, many of whom
claim blood relationship with their 'White cousins'. There was a
secondary strain of English intermarriage, especially in the areas of

George and Knysa, where the names MacKay, Martin, Dunn, Owen, Benn, and Bailey are not uncommon among Coloured families. The offspring of such intermarriages seldom find themselves fully accepted by their White relatives, while they themselves feel superior to their Coloured relatives: they needs must move in order to establish themselves as White. Today 60 per cent of the Cape Coloureds live in towns and cities, 25 per cent in Greater Cape Town alone.[24] Many live in the older, run-down parts of Cape Town, near the city centre, and along the railway line to the southern suburbs. Others live in recently established townships such as Athlone and Kensington, on the fringes of the city. According to the 1960 census report they slightly outnumber the Whites of Colander.

Such is the attraction of Colander to Coloured people that, while the numbers of White residents declined by about one-third between 1936 and 1960 (because, as one informant put it, 'The roof leaks, the Jew exploits, and I'm moving away from the skollies') the number of Coloureds increased in the same period by almost half. The proportion of Coloureds to the total population of Colander has risen steadily from approximately 30 per cent in 1936 to approximately 50 per cent in 1960.

Colander and its environs has for many years attracted 'better-class' Coloured residents. Its attraction for them is, in the first place, proximity to employment, for most Coloured housing estates, such as Bonteheuvel, are far from the factories of Colander which provide many Coloured persons with work. The income of most Coloureds is decidedly lower than that of most Whites, and the extra expense involved in travelling to work from these outlying areas is seen as a heavy burden. A second attraction of Colander is that rents, compared with other White areas, are low. But probably the greatest attraction of the district for Coloured persons, according to informants, is the fact that there White and Coloured housing intermingle. Whites and Coloureds live side by side as neighbours, though there is a tendency for the two groups to live on different sides of the same street, and a tendency for Coloureds to concentrate in densely populated pockets west of the main road. This intermingling provides an opportunity for relatively fair Coloured persons to acquire White status through residence in a nominally White area – one necessary condition of passing for White.

The reaction of Coloured people to those of their number who pass varies from the sympathetic to the hostile. There are those who give what help they can to passers and who dismiss the entire process airily as a justifiable means of circumventing economic discrimination: 'It's purely economic. If you can pass you can get a good job. We accept it. We don't think it's disloyal. It's necessity.' Yet others content themselves with bemoaning the loss of the pass-Whites to the Coloured community. Said a dubiously White Colander housewife: 'The cream of the Coloured people have left the country. There's lots left from here. They weren't used to it [the harsher discrimination practised since the Nationalist Party came to power]. They're all over now – Canada, England, America. . . . Is there any trouble in England? They make a very good impression. Only the scum is left.' On the other hand, denunciation and exposure to the White authorities is not uncommon. At one time an unofficial committee was formed among those property owners in the Colander area who had been ordered to move under the terms of the Group Areas Act with the express purpose of denouncing all their White relatives and all Whites whom they could prove had non-White blood. Hostility towards pass-Whites is particularly evident among the intellectual élite, which consists largely of younger, radical school teachers, some medical practitioners, and the majority of lawyers. These tend to despise passers as turncoats. Mr George Golding, President of the Coloured People's National Union, is quoted in the *Cape Times* as having said: 'I feel the Coloured people who, through subterfuge, have achieved White recognition, have "ratted" on their own people, instead of being in the fight to obtain full citizenship to which we are entitled, including the vote.'[25] Members of the élite also regard passers as upstarts: those who pass deny, by implication, the worth of the Coloured community, in which the élite have staked their all. Worse, it seems that a substantial proportion of those who pass occupy a status immediately below that of the élite, so that in the act of passing they leapfrog over the élite into the superordinate White group. From the point of view of members of the élite, pass-Whites are cheating not only in the sense that they assume, largely by virtue of their innate complexions, a superordinate status in relation to the élite without necessarily first acquiring the education and sophistication usually associated with élite status, but also in the sense that they are not playing the game according to the rules and entrenched values of the total society. Coloured businessmen (especially Muslims), white-collar workers, Protestant ministers of religion, and some of the older teachers (especially those with a rural background) are described by Coloured informants as conservative in their ways and as supporters of the government. Of them it might be said that, in the words of Sarah Gertrude Millin, 'To aspire to compete against the White man, to have dreams of drawing, in any respect, level with the White man, would seem almost a violation of nature.'[26] One Muslim businessman explained his thinking thus:

> The Coloured people lived in complete harmony with the Afrikaner until the Tommies came – the scum of society – miscegenated with them, debauched them, and taught them how to build slums. The Coloured people lost their race pride. They would not even speak their own language. So did the Bantu – they wanted to be Yanks. Now that the Nationalist Party has come the Coloured man has every opportunity to better himself. He does not have to start from scratch. He can follow in the path of the Whites, who is the boss in this country.

Pertinent here is Dickie-Clark's observation that

> The Coloureds' slight but valuable 'overlap' in the social dimension depends for its continuance on the maintenance of the domination of the Whites as a group. . . . Thus, despite the Coloured stratum's almost complete exclusion from the Whites, they yet have a stake in the maintenance of White rule.[27]

Those who pass during working hours but return to their families and friends at night, or at least at frequent intervals, appear to escape the full force of their relatives' enmity; indeed, they are likely to be given every assistance. This reaction might be interpreted as a reflection of that aspect of the White ethic which encourages the individual to exact maximum advantage within fair rules and to obtain the best employment he can. But those who cut themselves off completely from their relatives are likely to be regarded with varying degrees of hostility. Here is a case in point.

> The brothers Jannie and Piet are both of relatively fair complexion and possess European physiognomies. Piet, who is the fairer of the two, decided to pass, while, after a few humiliating experiments, Jannie decided otherwise. Jannie married an obviously Coloured woman and brought her to live in the paternal home in lower Colander. Piet married a woman of fair complexion, and moved to a house east of the main road, where there were more Whites, and cut himself off completely from his brother and other relatives. About two years ago, unbeknown to Jannie, he moved to a White suburb far from Colander and his old acquaintances.
>
> When the father died, Piet, the eldest, made arrangements for the funeral. Jannie offered to help, but his offer was brusquely refused. He was told to keep away from the ceremony, lest his brother be embarrassed. Nevertheless, he attended. Few were present, and, as it happened, there were not enough pall-bearers. Piet cast about himself in desperation but, though the need was pressing, deliberately overlooked his swarthy brother. After some hesitation Jannie wordlessly aligned himself with the other pall-bearers, and

carried his father to his grave. While the grave was yet open his brother accosted him, deeply angered. 'I thought we understood each other . . .' he hissed. So Jannie lost his temper and threatened to knock Piet into the grave. They broke up amid bitter recriminations.

Jannie despises his brother for cutting himself off from his family of origin and for assuming a form of speech and mannerism which is, allegedly, superciliously White. 'I can't talk to him any more,' he complained. 'We grew up together; but now he is White and I am not.' On the other hand, he has no objection to passing in some circumstances. He himself attends White cinemas and public houses and offers to fight anyone who challenges him. He has enrolled his own son at a White technical college. This son, after remaining at the college for only a few weeks, burst into the head-master's office and exclaimed, in a highly emotional state, 'I don't fit in here. I am Coloured. I want to leave.' When Jannie heard this he gave his son a severe beating for jeopardizing his chances of apprenticeship to a White trade.

But whether or not Coloureds approve of or resent those who pass, they invariably see the process as involving tragedy: 'The dark children go to Coloured school and the fair ones to a European school, and then they come home and sit together around the table. How can that be right? It's breaking up families. How can that be right? Why do they have to make a law?'

To sum up, this chapter reports the claim of informants that upward social mobility among Cape Coloureds can fruitfully be conceived as proceeding along a continuum at one end of which is the farm labourer and towards the other end of which occurs a bifurcation, one branch leading to élite status, the other to White status. Persons situated at the point of bifurcation may, if their complexion is sufficiently fair, choose to pass for White. The process of passing is facilitated by cultivating the ways of the White man, by leaving towns in which the passer's identity as a Coloured is known, and by moving to a district, such as Colander, where Whites and Coloureds intermingle. The act of passing evokes reactions among Coloured people varying from con-nivance to sharp antagonism.

NOTES

1 H. W. van der Merwe, *Social Stratification in a Cape Coloured Community*, M.A. thesis, University of Stellenbosch, 1957, p. 57.

2 S. Patterson, *Colour and Culture in South Africa*, London, Routledge and Kegan Paul, 1953.

3 S. P. Cilliers, *The Coloured People of South Africa*, Cape Town, Banier, 1963.

4 P. L. van den Berghe, *South Africa: A Study in Conflict*, Middletown, Wesleyan University Press, 1965.

5 *Report of the Commission of the Cape Coloured Population of the Union*, U.G. 54–1937.

6 S. P. Cilliers, *op. cit.*, Chapter 2.

7 S. Patterson, 1953, *op. cit.*, p. 167; H. W. van der Merwe, 1957, *op. cit.*, p. 90.

8 See H. F. Dickie-Clark, *The Marginal Situation*, London, Routledge and Kegan Paul, 1966, p. 91.

9 See H. W. van der Merwe, 1957, *op. cit.*, pp. 27–8. Some Coloured schools are thought to be 'snooty' because of their reputation for favouring fair-skinned applicants.

10 For an examination of racial discrimination in employment see G. V. Doxey, *The Industrial Colour Bar in South Africa*, London, Oxford University Press, 1961; R. Alexander and H. J. Simons, *Job Reservation and the Trade Unions*, Cape Town, Enterprise Press, 1959.

11 Census data are insufficiently precise to be used as a basis for calculations of this kind, especially since the number of Coloureds who pass for White is counter-balanced to an unknown extent by Bantu who pass for Coloured.

12 L. Green, *Outspan*, 17 November 1950, p. 19. An analysis of various other definitions of Coloured is made by S. Patterson, *op. cit.*, pp. 361–3.

13 See I. D. MacCrone, *Race Attitudes in South Africa*, Johannesburg, Witwatersrand University Press, 1957, Ch. III; J. S. Marais, *The Cape Coloured People*, Johannesburg, Witwatersrand University Press, 1957, Ch. I; Anon. 'The Origin and Incidence of Miscegenation at the Cape During the Dutch East India Company's Regime 1652–1795', in *Race Relations Journal*, Vol. XX, No. 2, 1953, pp. 23–7.

14 M. Jeffrys, 'Where do Coloureds Come From?', *Drum*, Nos. 102–6 and 108, 1959.

15 Van den Berghe, 1965, *op. cit.*, p. 42.

16 G. Findlay, *Miscegenation*, Pretoria, Pretoria News Publishers, 1936.

17 Hamilton Russell, M. P., *Cape Times*, 19 February 1963.

18 M. Horrell, *Race Classification in South Africa – Its Effects on Human Beings*, Johannesburg, South African Institute of Race Relations, 1958.

19 Some details have been altered in order to preserve anonymity.

20 See S. P. Cilliers, 1963, *op. cit.*, p. 27; Patterson, 1953, *op. cit.*, p. 163; Van der Merwe, 1957, *op. cit.*, p. 87. It is surely misleading to describe South Africa as a caste or caste-like society. The term caste focuses our attention upon barriers to inter-group mobility and blinds us to the kind of miscibility described here.

21 Migrations were deliberately planned for this purpose, but it is probable that, more often than not, this was just one of the factors taken into consideration when planning a move.

22 In the *Cape Times* of 4 April 1963, a member of the School Board is reported as advising the father of a dark-complexioned child to send his son to a school in the Transvaal, where it is easier for such a child to enrol in a White school.

23 *Cape Times*, 5 July 1961.

24 S. P. Cilliers, 1963, *op. cit.*, pp. 16–17. A map of the distribution of the Coloured population in South Africa can be found in M. Cole, *South Africa*, New York, Dutton, 1961, p. 663.

25 *Cape Times*, 3 August 1963.

26 S. H. Millin, *The People of South Africa*, New York, Knopf, 1954, p. 267.

27 H. F. Dickie-Clark, *op. cit.*, p. 154.

Chapter Three

PASSING FOR WHITE
IN SCHOOLS

Those who desire to pass commonly attempt to enrol in White schools. That many have succeeded in the attempt is a matter of fact. The commonly held belief that White and Coloured children have long been totally segregated in South African schools is erroneous for, as this chapter demonstrates, passing in White schools has been in evidence for many decades, and has persisted well into the Nationalist era in spite of vigorous attempts by successive governments to bring it to a halt. Many White schools in Cape Town have, in recent years, been reclassified as Coloured schools because they accepted so many pass–White pupils. It is against this background that the phenomenon of pass–Whites at Colander High School must be seen.

The schooling of White children in the Cape Province is overwhelmingly a provision of the State, though there are some private schools still under the tutelage of the churches. Coloured schools, on the other hand, are very largely denominational Mission Schools (in 1961 there were 140 Coloured schools under School Boards and 1,248 Mission Schools for Coloureds in the Cape),[1] though such schools are now increasingly coming under the guardianship of the Public School Boards. The division of responsibility for schooling between the State and the churches has had profound ramifications for education in South Africa, especially since the churches, Anglican, Wesleyan, and Dutch Reformed – and the missionary societies, such as the Glasgow Missionary Society – have concerned themselves largely with the schooling of non-Whites. The division of responsibility is an old one and represents the first important step in the process of racial segregation in the schools in South Africa.

The Education Act of 1865 drew a distinction between undenominational public schools, controlled by local committees of management; denominational Mission Schools, under the control of a church or missionary body; and schools for *natives*. It provided that public schools were subsidized on the pound-for-pound principle, but that Mission Schools and Native Schools received scaled grants.[2] Thus only that section of the population which could afford to maintain its own schools – the White section – could send its children to public schools. Coloured children and the poorer White children went to Mission Schools.

This Act consolidated the trend, already apparent for some time, of racial segregation in schools. Public schools had long provided for most of the White children of the Cape Colony, while Mission Schools, although patronized by a number of White children, were attended largely by Coloured pupils. In evidence laid before the Education Commission of 1863, the Rev. Mr Faure claimed that the public schools and the Mission Schools had '. . . practically become separate schools for the white and the blacks'.[3]

The Act did not complete the segregation of White and Coloured pupils: aided Mission Schools were intended to provide schooling for the 'poorer classes', White as well as Coloured. In 1883, Ross found nearly six thousand Whites in the same classrooms as 32,000 Coloured children in the Mission Schools.[4] In 1891 there were still over ten thousand White children in Mission Schools,[5] a figure which represented almost one-third of the total White enrolment in the Colony. According to evidence set before the Education Commission of 1892,[6] there were at the time twenty-five Mission Schools in Cape Town, attended by 'practically three thousand white children and 4,283 coloured'.[7] Even during the earlier years of the twentieth century, the Mission School Zonnebloem had an enrolment half of which consisted of Africans, the other half being White and Coloured.[8]

Although it was not unusual for some Coloured pupils to be enrolled in the non-denominational public schools in the towns, the complaint of the times was not that Coloureds were intruding on White schools, but that Whites were pushing the Coloureds out of their Mission Schools. This led, in 1892, to a counter-protest which rings strangely in contemporary South African ears: 'I do not think there should be anything to exclude white children from a coloured school, if the parents are respectable, and they are clean and properly clothed . . .'[9]

So it can be seen that, by 1892, the leaders of the English-medium churches and government officials possessed divergent views on 'mixed' schooling. The English churches have throughout consistently remained relatively liberal in their attitude – in February 1958 the Anglican Synod of the Diocese of Cape Town unanimously adopted a resolution supporting the establishment of a mixed Coloured and

White school.[10] The present-day government, on the other hand, would not seriously quarrel with Sir Langham Dale, who, as Superintendent-General of Education for the Colony, said before the Education Commission of 1892,[11] 'I do not consider it my business to force education on all the aborigines; it would mean ruin to South Africa. If I could produce 60,000 educated Tembus or Fingoes tomorrow, what would you do with them?; their education must be gradual.'

The debate that took place before the Education Commission of 1892 was so portentous for South Africa, so striking in its similarities – and dissimilarities – to the debate that rages today, that it is worth citing at length. Sir Langham Dale is being questioned about the proposed fourth-class schools, the purpose of which is 'to take the White children out from among the Coloured classes'. Punctuation and paragraphing are as in the original.

Dr Berry: Do you propose to give the Managers power to exclude coloured children, because there is the difficulty of spoiling the school by the introduction of the coloured element. Would it not be advisable to give the Managers power to regulate who are to be the scholars and who are not? – That is a dangerous power to put into an Act of Parliament, as many off-coloured children in Cape Town consider themselves white. I have had to deal with these difficulties now for more than 30 years, and it is curious how they all vanish in practice.

Apparently they do not vanish. These Mission Schools were established for coloured children, and the white children have evicted them? – The white children have pressed into them because there is no other place for them to go to.

President: Is there not the danger of the coloured children pressing into the white schools? – I do not think so; the fees would be four times as much, in the first place.

But many of the coloured parents are very well off, and they would not look to that. They have already had their children with white children and they would not like to be thrust back? – I think it would be just the other way; the coloured people complain that they are pushed out.

But it is desirable that they should go? – Yes.

Then if it is desirable that they should go, why should not the Government lay down a rule that they should not go to the schools intended for whites? – I do not think the Government would take the responsibility of saying who is Malay and who is a coloured person.

Dr Berry: The thing is this, if you have a fourth class school, you have a number of whites and a very few coloured children. In the mission schools you have a preponderance of blacks, and the coloured children will generally

D

go where you have many coloured, and the whites will go just as they do in the undenominational schools at present. That is the only safeguard you have that the mixture would not be so great? – The serious objection is to the mixture of the so-called Street Arab with the white girls.[12]

In 1893, Proclamation 388 made it possible in certain circumstances for White Mission Schools to be established in various centres. These were *Poor Schools*, established to withdraw White children from the Mission Schools,[13] and which were ultimately to be absorbed into the ordinary nondenominational public schools. This was thought proper because, as Sir Langham Dale said, 'It is very undesirable that White children, especially the girls, should be brought into close relations with the ordinary type of Coloured street boy.'[14] In the following year, in the *Report of the Superintendent-General for 1894*, there was for the first time a distinction made between White and Coloured children in school statistics.

In 1905 the School Board Act was passed, and School Boards then took the place of the old Committees of Management. It became the duty of School Boards to establish non-denominational public schools and to maintain control over them. The Act also provided for the establishment of schools for pupils of 'other than European parentage or extraction'. Boards could apply for the enforcement of compulsory education for all White children between the ages of seven and fourteen. Prior to the passing of this Act, the parents of a Coloured child could insist that the child was admitted to a nondenominational public school. After the passing of the Act, it became very difficult for a Coloured child to be educated other than in a Mission School, where he did not proceed beyond the fourth standard.[15] True, the Act did not expressly exclude non-Whites from White schools, but this interpretation was later laid upon it in the Courts.[16] The judgement was, however, mitigated by the ruling that school committees were not compelled to inquire into the descent of a child seeking admission to a school for Whites if it was not obvious from appearance that the child was of other than European descent. School managers could, if they wished, wink at the admission of pass-Whites. Many did. By the time of Union, according to the Education Commission of 1912,[17] there were less than 550 European pupils in Mission Schools, yet the *Cape School Board Report* of 1934 attributes the large increase in school enrolment up to 1914 as 'partly due to the transfer of 1,000 European pupils from Coloured Mission Schools to European Schools'.

In spite of discriminatory legislation, many Coloured children, especially those who were of fair complexion, continued to attend

White schools. They could not legally have done so without the consent of the School Board and of School Committees for, while the Cape Provincial Department of Education exercises general control over professional and financial matters in State schools, School Boards (the majority of whose officers are elected by voters on a Divisional Council or Municipal roll) are responsible for seeing that the rules regarding compulsory school attendance are enforced and local School Committees (consisting of persons elected by parents who have one or more children on the roll of the local school) admit or exclude pupils. [18]

The consent of the School Board to the enrolment of pass-Whites appears to have been obtained, for according to the School Board minutes of 2 March 1932: '. . . When the Arsenal Road [Simonstown] School was established by the Board, it was understood that the School should make provision for such [almost White] children as well as for those of pure European descent.' A School Board official claimed that this school was 'high grade', with 'good uniforms and books', and that it was intended to cater for 'better-class borderline pupils'. In the same School Board minutes is reported the proposal by the Board, submitted to the Department, that both White and Coloured pupils be allowed to attend Silo School (Simonstown). The Superintendent replied that the proposal was contrary to law. A preceding passage in the School Board minutes implicates School Committees: 'In many schools for European pupils there are a number of children who are not of pure European descent, but who might pass as Europeans, more especially in schools in which there is a desire on the part of the local Committee and Principal to increase the number of pupils . . .' And the Secretary of the School Board, in his *Report on the Problem Regarding the Non-admission of Pupils to European Schools in the Cape Peninsula* (*circa* 1943), writes, with regard to some pupils expelled from White schools: '. . . the Board had already taken strenuous steps to improve the position. Meetings had actually been held with the local Committees to impress upon them the necessity for exercising great care in admitting new children to school.' So it is clear that in at least some White schools pass-Whites gained admission with the connivance of the School Committees. [19]

Even the Department of Education was not always prepared to draw the line between White and Coloured very sharply. In January 1938, the Department wrote to the Cape School Board in these terms:

> Once it is clear that a child is not European it is illegal to admit it to a school for Europeans. It is a matter for policy whether the eyes should be closed to

any such cases. If and when application is made for admission of a second or third child, own brother or sister of a child already admitted, it becomes clear that one or other parents is not of unmixed European parentage or extraction, then legally all the children must be excluded. However, if it is a borderline case and one or more children have already attended school for a considerable time it would be more equitable to leave them.

The Cape School Board regarded itself as still bound by this ruling until the end of 1957, and some School Committees continued to act as if the ruling remained valid in the 1960s.

An earlier administration was less charitable. In February 1932, the Superintendent-General of Education informed the Cape School Board that no provision was made in the Ordinance for 'slightly Coloured' children, and said that any such cases must be classified as Coloured and sent to a Coloured school since, in the judgement of Lord de Villiers, 'European parentage or extraction' meant unmixed 'European parentage or extraction'.[20] Moreover, the Board's attention was drawn to the fact that the Arsenal Road School (a White school which had been admitting pass-Whites) was graded by the Department as a European school, the teachers were paid salaries as though the school were a European school, and the Province drew a subsidy on the basis of the school's being a European school. The Board was asked to furnish the Department of Education with a statement regarding any of the schools under its control professedly set apart for Whites to which pupils known to be 'slightly Coloured' had been admitted.

There were at least five so-called 'buffer schools' catering for 'borderline cases'[21]: Arsenal Road, Simonstown; Broad Road, Wynberg; Sydney Street, Cape Town; East Park Primary; and Anderdale Primary. A senior official of the Board told me that 'When these children that we tried to pretend didn't exist came to us we said: "Why not try Broad Road or Sydney Street?" ' 'Buffer schools' such as these existed, according to the previously mentioned report to the School Board, 'without the sanction of the authorities but with no direct interference from them.' In contradistinction to this assertion, a most reliable informant told me categorically that these schools were set up by the Superintendent-General, at the request of teachers' organizations, quite explicitly to cater for 'borderline cases'.

In 1934, 'as the Department insisted on a more rigid interpretation of the term European descent in terms of the law',[22] the Cape School Board converted three schools, Broad Road, Sydney Street, and Arsenal Road, from European to Coloured, removing the Europeans elsewhere. This involved the transfer of some thirty pupils from the

Arsenal Road school. In the two other schools there was practically no transfer of pupils necessitated by the change.

The closure of these schools as White schools was recommended by a sub-committee of the Board, whose report on the matter concludes with the words: 'As for the rest [other White schools which had admitted "slightly Coloured" pupils] your Committee are of opinion that drastic action at this juncture is impracticable and might lead to justifiable opposition.'[23]

A few years later it was discovered that certain other schools would also have to be changed, and the closing of some of these as White schools only served to make matters more difficult for the Board. East Park School (Cape Town) was closed as a White school, as was Anderdale Primary, and the portion of the children who were European transferred to other schools.

As a result of the Department's decision to take action in one instance,[24] the school Principal and the School Committee, after investigating each child, evicted more than seventy children – that is, more than one-third of the enrolment – from the school. The Department then established a Coloured school at Newlands to house these children, but only 25 of the 70 were admitted. No record of what happened to the remaining 45 is available. After three years this school closed down altogether, and the parents refused to send their children to a school where they would have to associate with Coloured children.

In 1940 the relevant rules regarding the admission of pupils to European schools were amended, thus:

It shall be the duty of the principal teacher and the committee of any school set apart for pupils of European parentage or extraction to satisfy themselves that the school is being attended only by such pupils; and the committee shall exclude from the school any pupils whom it considers not to be of European parentage or extraction.

It shall be the duty of the board to satisfy itself that the committees of the schools under its jurisdiction set apart for pupils of European parentage or extraction are carrying out the provision of these rules.

Appeal from the decision of the committee, whether such decision relates to the admission, the retention or the exclusion of a child from the school, shall be made to the board concerned and, similarly, appeal from the decision of a board shall be made to the Superintendent-General of Education.

It shall be competent for a committee or a board of the Superintendent-General of Education to require proof of the European parentage or extraction of a child; and the onus of such proof shall lie on the parent of such child.[25]

No doubt at all was left as to what procedure should be followed; and in any doubtful cases the onus of proving themselves of 'European parentage or extraction' lay clearly with the parents of the child. Moreover, it became the duty of the Principal and the Committee and the Board not only to exercise great care in admitting pupils to their schools, but also to exercise care regarding pupils already enrolled.

As a result of these amendments to the regulations, some 30 pupils were excluded from three primary schools at Parow, near Cape Town. Here, again, a new Coloured school was commenced, in a hired building, for those so eliminated. The opening enrolment was 26 – three years later there were only 12 pupils in the school. The Raymond Primary School at Vasco excluded 25 children, some of whom had been attending the school for five or six years.

These amendments did not bring the Board's problems to an end. In Cape School Board Annual Reports of the forties and fifties[26] it is asserted that a great deal of the Board's time was taken up with 'non-admission cases'. Especially loud complaints were made in 1952 when 'the position regarding such non-admission cases became more acute than ever' and in 1958 when 'The Board found even greater difficulty than in the past in dealing with such cases under the terms of the 1956 Education Ordinance'. A further report on the problem was submitted to the Board on 1 December 1957. It noted that '. . . a large number of Coloured pupils have been enrolled to European schools'. The 1962 Report indicates that the Board dealt with thirty-nine 'non-admission cases' during the year.

After 1940 the Board continued converting White schools into Coloured schools. When the Salt River Primary (Dryden Street) was closed as a European school in 1952, 341 pupils left. The Cape School Board states that 111 of the 341 pupils were obviously of 'European parentage or extraction', and these were admitted to the Victoria Walk Primary, Woodstock; 43 of the remaining 230 applied for admission to White schools. Thirteen were admitted to Victoria Walk after investigations of the School Board, and the other 30 applicants were rejected. Applications were not received by the Board from the remaining 187 pupils.[27]

Between 1932 and 1956 at least fourteen White non-denominational schools under School Boards in the Cape Peninsula were reclassified

Coloured. All these schools were situated in areas which were once White residential areas but are now predominantly Coloured, and all are known to have accepted at least some pass-Whites. Of six of them it can be said with assurance that a major reason for their reclassification was the fact that they had accepted so many pass-Whites.

It may be that these schools represent only the tip of the iceberg. The schools we have discussed so far have all been public schools, not private church schools. Yet these Roman Catholic, Anglican, and Methodist church schools are reputed to have accepted pass-Whites more readily than State schools. Unfortunately, no records of relevance have been made public. In addition to established church schools, transient fee-paying nondenominational schools, set up especially to cater for pass-Whites who had experienced difficulty in enrolling in State schools, are known to have mushroomed for a period all over the Peninsula. One such 'marginal' school in Woodstock was closed in May 1953. In the School Board minutes of 1 July of that year it is stated that the parents of the children enrolled in the school were notified that before their children could be admitted to a White school the 'usual documentary proof of pure European parentage and extrac-tion would have to be furnished. Replies had been received from some 15 parents, but no replies had been received from approximately 50 of the families.'[28]

This then is the background against which the phenomenon of pass-Whites at Colander High School must be viewed. How the school attempts to cope with it is described in the next chapter.

NOTES

1 *Report of the Superintendent-General of Education (Cape)*, 1961.

2 *Cape of Good Hope: Annexures to Votes and Proceedings of the Legislative Council for 1865*, Section entitled 'Code of School Regulations'.

3 *Education Commission, 1861 (Cape of Good Hope). Minutes of Evidence*, p. 152 (G. 24–63).

4 D. Ross, *Preliminary Report on the State of Education in the Cape of Good Hope, 1883* (G. 12–83).

5 See *Report of the Superintendent-General of Education, 1909*, p. 6.

6 *Education Commission, 1892, First Report*, p. 152 (G. 9–91).

7 This called forth the comment: 'The difficulty is to distinguish who are 'coloured' children. I should think the distribution of White and Coloured just mentioned is a very arbitrary one.'

8 *The Story of Zonnebloem*, broadcast by the South African Broadcasting

Corporation, 2 March 1958. Transcript deposited at the South African Public Library. See also, 'Mixed Schooling in South African History', by R. W. H. Shepherd, in *Cape Times*, 27 February 1958. A school not unlike Zonnebloem, in the Eastern Cape, is the subject of *Lovedale Past and Present*, Lovedale, Mission Press, 1887.

9 Rev. H. Tindall, in *Education Commission, 1892, First Report* (G. 9–91), p. 127.

10 It is interesting to note that the Afrikaans churches were not always opposed to this policy. See *Education Commission, 1892, First Report, op. cit.*, p. 13: 'There is a very large mission at Bree Street, belonging to the Dutch Reformed Church, and there are two-thirds White children, and one-third Malay and Coloured people . . .'

11 *Education Commission, 1892, Third Report*, p. 32.

12 *Ibid;* p. 16 paras. 115–24.

13 *Ibid.*, p. 4.

14 See *Report of the Interdepartmental Committee on Native Education, 1935* (U.G. No. 29/1936).

15 See C. de K. Fowler, *School Administration*, Cape Town, Maskew Miller, 1953.

16 *Moller vs. Keimoes School Committee and Another*, C.P.D. 1911, p. 673. Upheld on appeal A.D. 1911, p. 635.

17 *Cape of Good Hope Education Commission*, 1912 (C.P. 6–1912).

18 School administration in the Cape Province is lucidly discussed by C. de K. Fowler, *ibid.*

19 That a parallel situation may have developed in Southern Rhodesia is indicated in C. A. Rogers and C. Frantz, *Racial Themes in Southern Rhodesia*, New Haven, Yale University Press, 1962, p. 2831: 'Some school teachers also speak knowingly about the number of children in their schools who "pass for White" although their neighbours are not always unaware of their ancestry.'

20 Keimoes Case, *op. cit.*

21 Dickie-Clark, 1966, *op. cit.*, p. 60, draws attention to such a school in Durban. 'Special schools' for mestizos in the United States are discussed in B. Berry, *Almost White*, New York, Macmillan, 1963, Ch. 8.

22 Cape School Board *Annual Report*, 1932.

23 *School Board Minutes*, 6/7/32: 'Reports of the Special Committee Regarding the Admission of Slightly Coloured Pupils to Schools'. Similar extensive reports are recorded in the Minutes of 6/7/38; 2/8/39; 6/3/40; 1/12/57.

24 1940. Feldhausen Primary, now Grove Primary.

25 'Rules Regarding Pupils in European Schools and Students in European Training Colleges', as published in the *Education Gazette*, 23 May 1940. This clarifies the position as outlined in the Rules published on 14 August 1924. No changes in substance are in the subsequent amendments of 30 July 1942; 1 November 1945; and 29 November 1956; but on 30 May 1957 significant changes were made regarding student teachers in training colleges (subsequently further amended); and in 1963 it was laid down that a child should be accepted at

a White school if both parents had White identity cards and if the child's birth certificate described him as White.

26 1942, 1947, 1948, 1949, 1952, 1953, 1954, 1955, 1956.

27 *Records of the Provincial Council*, 5 March 1954.

28 See also reports in the *Cape Argus*, 22 June 1953, and in the *Cape Times*, 3 December 1953.

Chapter Four

PASSING FOR WHITE IN COLANDER HIGH SCHOOL

Colander High School is a 'buffer school' and ever since its inception it has had to contend with 'borderline cases'.[1] How did it cope? Until the amendment in 1963, to the regulations concerning the admission of pupils, the Principal scrutinized each child applying for admission to his school together with a parent (usually the mother) at a preliminary interview. If both parents were in appearance obviously White the child might be admitted, provided there was a place for him,[2] and he was not in other ways unsuitable. If one or the other was obviously Coloured in appearance, admission was refused. In case of doubt the child and both parents were interviewed by the School Committee, sitting with the Principal, who attempted to establish the race of the child. Should they refuse the child, the parents had the right of appeal to the School Board, then to the Superintendent-General of Education, and from him to the Supreme Court.

How was the race of a 'borderline' child established? The answer is not a simple one, for the Superintendent-General, prior to 1963, was not bound by the decision of the Director of Census and Statistics, and, indeed, the touchstone of Whiteness employed by him was even more demanding than that used by the Director.

The Education Ordinance of 1921 laid down that the onus was on the parents to prove that they were of 'European parentage or extraction'. In the Ordinance of 1956 the definition of European was brought into line with that of the Population Registration Act, viz: 'European means a person who in appearance obviously is, or is generally accepted as, a White person, but does not include a person who, although in appearance obviously a White person, is generally accepted as a Coloured person.' Officials of the Department of Education say that the point of the revised definition in the Ordinance was that the burden of deciding difficult cases for admission should no longer fall on the shoulders of the Department, but should fall into line with classifications made under the Population Registration Act. But it was still up to the Superintendent-General to decide, once the classification had been made by the Director of Census and Statistics, whether or not he agreed with the ruling for educational purposes. No provision existed under either the 1921 or the 1956 Ordinances to enable the Superintendent-General to delegate to some other person or body his duty of deciding an appeal on race classification from the School Board. He is explicitly empowered by the Education Ordinance of 1956 (p. 104) to 'make rules governing the admission, enrolment, attendance, transfer, withdrawal, exclusion and expulsion of pupils in any schools (other than training colleges) for European pupils'. The final say regarding the admission of children to White schools rested therefore with him (subject to appeal to the Supreme Court) and not with the Director of Census and Statistics.

The Administrator said in the Provincial Council in June 1959 that if parents held White identity cards, then, as a general rule, their children would be admitted to White schools, though if a child of parents holding White identity cards associated more with Coloured children than with White, no harm would be done by sending this child to a Coloured school. A senior official of the Cape School Board suggested 'off the record' that the real reason why the Department was not necessarily prepared to accept a child both of whose parents had White identity cards was that the child might be a 'throwback' and appear 'obviously Coloured'. It appears that the Department wished to leave itself a loophole should a child whose parents satisfied the requirements of the Population Registration Act be nevertheless considered an undesirable pupil through association with Coloured children.

The Minister of the Interior, in reply to the second reading of the Population Registration Bill, said in the House on 16 March 1950[3] that 'The test [for a White person] that is laid down in this Bill is the test of appearance and of usual associations. There is no question of descent or of blood.' But, according to Mrs C. Taylor, sometime member of the Cape School Board and of the Cape Provincial Council,

In a letter addressed to the legal advisers of a man whose case has been considered, the Superintendent-General of Education said on November 8 [1956]: 'While I do not feel called upon to discuss with you what factors are to be borne in mind in determining these cases, I would state that I am aware of the leading decisions of our courts, including those to the effect that descent is the test and that appearance, whatever its probative value, like other factors, may afford evidence of descent.' There is no mention here of association.[4]

The retention of the criterion of extraction was made even more clear in instructions given to the Board by the Department in April 1956:

... I have to say that in terms of the Department's rules regarding the admission of pupils to schools for European pupils, the onus of proof of the European parentage or extraction of a child lies on the parent of such child.

While it is difficult to catalogue all the factors that a school committee or board should take into consideration in order to reach a decision whether a particular child may be admitted to a school for European pupils, the following are of importance
(a) the appearance of the child
(b) the appearance of the parents, the schools they attended, whether they live with Europeans or amongst Coloured, whether they associate with Europeans or with Coloureds, the capacity in which the father is employed;
(c) whether the grandparents of the child are/were in each case accepted as Europeans.

The parents should be asked *inter alia* to submit their own birth and marriage certificates and those of the grandparents.[5]

Thus it would appear that, while the Director of Census and Statistics requires merely that a person should appear White and be accepted as White before bestowing upon him the benefits of a White identity card, the Superintendent-General, using the same definition of a White person, required not only that these conditions should be met before admitting a child to a White school, but also that the parents of such a child should establish his 'White parentage or extraction' and that parents should be asked for their birth and marriage certificates, and for those of the grandparents.[6] School Committees followed his lead and inquired into ancestry.

How did the School Committee of Colander High decide on the classification of 'doubtful cases'? Where such cases were referred to the School Committee by the Principal, they invited both parents and their child (or children) to an interview. Should either parent not have attended this interview, the child was almost automatically refused admission, it being assumed that the non-attendance of one parent was an admission that he or she was not White. Should both parents have attended they might have been required to furnish birth certificates, and to supplement these by statements by people of standing in the community to the effect that they were normally accepted as Whites. Committee members also made use of their own personal knowledge of the area in an attempt to assay the race of applicants for admission to the school.

These interviews were held in camera, so it is not possible to say with confidence on what basis children were classified by the School Committee. Some indication is, however, given by Committee minutes and correspondence between the Principal and the School Board.

Of the 207 applicants who were refused admission to the school during two recent years on the grounds of colour, 7 were rejected because one or more of the parents did not present themselves before the Committee, while the remaining 13 had appended to his or her name the comments, 'appearance against', 'appearance unfavourable', or 'appearance not acceptable'. Additional reasons were cited in nine cases: 'previous members of family were refused' (3); 'appearance of father' [or mother] (2); 'outside our area' and 'living in predominantly non-European area' (3); and 'brother unsatisfactory'. It should be emphasized that these are merely the reasons which the school administrators have chosen to put in black and white (albeit *sub rosa*), and that they might or might not be the real reasons.

Prior to 1963 disagreement obtained between Committee members on the classification of children. Of the twenty decisions to reject a child, discussed above, only ten were unanimous. These decisions concerned the children whose parents did not present themselves before the Committee, those who 'lived outside our area', and one whose brother was 'unsatisfactory'. Eight decisions were recorded as 'almost unanimous' or as carried with a majority of five or six out of seven. One case, which concerned brothers, one of whom was described as 'passable' and the other as 'not acceptable', resulted in a three-four split. The voting on the remaining instance is not recorded.

It might be noted that each of these rejected children attended local White primary schools, and that three of them had been enrolled in nearby White high schools, and that another three had siblings who had been, or who were at the time, enrolled at Colander High.

Reliable figures concerning the number of children refused admission on the grounds of colour are not available but, according to the same source of information, and subject to the same qualifications, the numbers rejected for the years 1952–1959 were:

1952	35	1956	14
1953	94	1957	?
1954	27	1958	9
1955	25	1959	11

Disagreement obtained about the classification of children not only between the Committee members themselves but also between the Committee and the School Board. There exists, in the form of correspondence from the School Board, a record of the appeals of two of the children rejected in one recent year, both of whom were described as 'appearance unsatisfactory'.

Case A
It is noted that his brother is already enrolled at your school. Although he is dark complexioned, the Board had, from very careful investigations established at an interview with the Rev. X that the father, now deceased, was employed as a European. The family is very closely linked with church activities. Would you now accept . . . ?

Case B
As a result of investigations made and after an interview with the parents, when both sons were present, the Board decided that B is dark but both parents are in possession of European birth certificates, and as far as the Board has been able to establish, the family has European associations. The children also attend the Presbyterian Sunday School. Under the circumstances I am directed to ask whether you would now be prepared to admit B to your school.

The number of appeals from the Colander High Committee to the Board or to the Superintendent-General, during that or any other year, is not disclosed, but it is certainly small, if only because of the considerable legal expenses which the financially poor parents would incur if they pressed their case with any vigour, and because the procedure is, in any case, not without its risks. The moment the Department asks the Director of Census and Statistics for information about an appellant there exists, by implication, a doubt about the appellant's classification in terms of the Population Registration Act. This would have more widespread effects on the appellant than an obligation to change schools. That being so, the Director, acting under Section 5 (3) of the Population Registration Act, is empowered to initiate an inquiry into the race of the appellant and to alter, without giving reasons, any classification he had already made. Moreover, the parents of rejectees, whether they have been summoned before the Committee or not, are not informed of the real reason for their rejection – they are normally told simply that the school is full. Not even the School Board – to whom the Principal has been instructed to disclose the reason for each refusal – is told unequivocally that a child has been refused on the grounds of colour: in correspondence addressed to the Board the Principal covers himself by claiming that 'In the first instance, inability to accommodate is the reason for refusal.' In answer to verbal queries from the Board the Principal is reticent. 'He led me to the brink,' he said, recounting his response to such a query, 'but I wouldn't say it. I told him we were full up with thirty or forty in each classroom and we weren't prepared to take anyone until we got an increase of staff. Mind you, he must have taken one look at the boy and seen there was less milk than coffee and known perfectly well that wasn't my reason, but he couldn't say so.'

The reason for such reticence on the part of the Principal and Committee is that appeals to the Board are (they say) so often successful – so often that, according to a senior official of the Board, the Board was 'deeply suspect by the authorities'. This has had the effect of lessening the confidence of parents in the Committee, and of lowering the morale of the Committee itself. The effect is exacerbated when, as has occasionally happened, the rulings given by the Board are inconsistent with one another. In one case, the Board, having rejected the appeal from the decision of the Committee of one boy of dark complexion and St Helena descent, later forced the Principal to accept his sister, who had already been refused admission to 'all' White schools within and without reasonable distance of her home.

The success of such appeals has led to a certain amount of friction between the Board and various School Committees. Principals have sometimes refused to take a child into a White school in spite of instructions from the Board.[8]

The success of such appeals has led also to the enrolment at Colander High of some of the darkest children in the school. Complained the Principal, 'There are some children who should never be here. They are the wrong type, and they affect the others. But I can do nothing. All the darkest children I have here have been forced on me by the Board.'

Many appeals concerning the decisions of School Committees in the Cape Peninsula do in fact reach the Cape School Board. In answer to a question put to the School Board and to the Department by a member of the Provincial Council on the author's behalf, it was claimed that from 1950 to 1960, inclusive, 'roughly 50' appeals reached the Board. How many were granted is not disclosed. The same sources state that appeals from the Board's decision to the Superintendent-General numbered 'not more than one or two per year'. Again, the number of successful appeals is not disclosed. I am told that a very large number of appeals are settled over the telephone and are never officially recorded.

When identity cards came into general use in the late 1950s controversy diminished at Colander High School. Few who were not in possession of White cards applied for admission to the school and so fewer 'doubtful' cases had to be considered by the School Committee. The problem presented by parents who had not understood instructions, who had not produced adequate documentary evidence as to their Whiteness, or whose progenitors could not be traced, was largely obviated. Moreover, the Board appeared to have been insisting that all children whose parents were in possession of White cards be accepted. The School Committee thus considered themselves very largely relieved of a source of great embarrassment and dissension, which in the past had led to resignations from among their number, and to a great deal of personal unpopularity.

Since an 'objective' criterion for admission was established, the vituperation once heaped upon the School Committee and the Principal of Colander High has been deflected on to the shoulders of those responsible for the framing of the regulations. The Principal is now able to say, with some satisfaction, 'There are those who say it is a rotten school and go on saying it: they become vindictive; they hate my guts. I don't blame them, really. But the vindictiveness is slowly being directed towards the Department rather than me nowadays as people know that it is the law rather than me personally. I can talk to them now: the law demands this. . . .'

Yet in spite of the manifest attractions of basing decisions entirely on the possession of White identity cards, the Principal and School Committee still reject children on the grounds of appearance alone.[9] As we have seen, many persons of dusky complexions are in possession of White identity cards. This has led to the enrolment of dark children to Colander High who in former years would have been refused admission. But in the case of very dark children the Principal still puts his foot down and refuses to admit the child. 'I had Coloureds in here,' he said, 'and as soon as they came in the door I sent them out the door. Black as the Ace of Spades, and they're living with Coloureds. "But," he said, "I've got a White ticket and I want my son in a White school." Goodness only knows where they get them. Came from a Coloured school. Some have even been to Standard Seven in a Coloured school and want to get into my Standard Eight.'

Whether or not to accept such children is still – in fact, if not in theory – largely a matter for the Principal's discretion. Said one school Principal, 'I have now a dozen children in my school who on paper are non-White, but who, by association, are White in every respect.' But he remained concerned about swarthy complexions: 'I can accept that child,' he said, 'but what do I do when I have a school function and the rest of the family comes along?'[10]

Just as it remains largely a matter for the discretion of a Principal to reject children with White papers but dusky complexions, so is it a matter for his discretion to accept children who lack White papers (but do not have Coloured papers) and are of fair complexion. Here is an illustration. In the early 1950s the first of three daughters of a White father and a Coloured mother was admitted to Colander High without having been asked to produce her birth certificate for she was White in appearance. The fact that her mother was Coloured was discovered by a Cape School Board Attendance Officer when he investigated the absence from school of the youngest daughter. The child was not removed from the school though the Attendance Officer threatened her that if she did not attend school regularly he would 'ask for [her] identity papers'.

School Committees seem less concerned with the letter of the law than is the Board (they are not so concerned with 'parentage or extraction') but they are more insistent than is the Board that a child of 'doubtful' appearance shall not be admitted to their schools.

It seems likely, though it cannot be established with any certainty, that the School Committee of Colander High is even more fearful of admitting swarthy children than are the committees of most other schools. At least some children who have been refused entry to Colander High have eventually been enrolled in other schools, such as the South African College Boys' High School, of considerably higher social standing. It is said that such schools, long before the amendment of 1963, were accepting White identity cards at their face value, while the Principal of Colander High still turned away 'doubtful cases', 'white ticket' or no 'white ticket', because 'I don't want the school to get the reputation'.

Such is the Principal's determination to exclude dark children that he is prepared to court considerable friction between himself and his feeder schools. A search through the records of school correspondence reveals a profusion of memoranda addressed to the Department and to the Board complaining that his feeder schools were accepting children of penumbral complexion. In the 1940s he wrote that he felt it unjust that he should be 'put into the position of having to refuse pupils into secondary standards who have already been four or five years in a so-called European school. . . . I strongly urge the Department to look into this matter in respect of our primary schools so that the terrible

E

injustice and humiliation now inflicted upon so many innocent lives shall be avoided.'[11]

The Principal is prepared to alienate not only the Board and his feeder school, but also Coloured residents of Colander. When the Western Province Land Tenure Advisory Board deliberated upon the future Group Areas zoning of Colander, he sent a teacher to represent the interests of the school. This is his account of the proceedings:

> They were going to zone what obviously looked a Coloured area Coloured. They said if the majority are Coloured then it is a Coloured area. Mr X [the teacher] said, 'Are you going to contradict your own census returns?' [which only just gave the Whites the edge over the Coloureds] - so they zoned it White. When I heard that I said 'Hooray! the school is saved!'

The Principal's delight at this decision is echoed by the other teachers: 'From our point of view the Group Areas Act was a godsend. It'll turf out some Coloureds, damn dagoes, and fishermen, Syrians – and they're not up to much – and Portuguese types.'

But for all that, wails the Principal, 'It's made very little difference. The Board still sends me Coloured children. And once they've got their cards there is no arguing with them.'

It would appear, then, that the Principal is less liberal in his interpretation of what constitutes a White person than is the Department, the Board, the Director of Census and Statistics, the Western Province Land Tenure Advisory Board, his feeder schools, and, probably, many schools in Cape Town. This is not because he is a man without liberal inclinations. He is conscious of the humiliations and deprivations attendant upon government policy. He is troubled by the role he is called upon to play as an arbiter of the race of a child. Why then is he so insistent on the exclusion of 'borderline' children?

The Board has to administer a school system according to bureaucratic regulations; the consequences of these regulations do not affect them as intimately as they do the staff and School Committee of Colander High; the school Principal is therefore called upon to exercise comparatively greater vigilance than the Board. To the Board the admission of a dark child to a White school means, perhaps, little more than a tick beside yet another name on yet another piece of paper; at most it means that they have succeeded in solving the difficult problem of enrolling the child at a school, as they are legally bound to do. For them there the matter rests. For the Principal, however, the child represents a sinister threat to the White status of his school, to his

ability to attract teachers and pupils of sufficient number and satis-
factory quality, and, ultimately, to his own personal prestige.

The teachers of Colander High are aware that in recent years a
number of White schools in the area have been reclassified as Coloured
'because the Principals were so kind-hearted'. Rumours continually
circulate to the effect that the same fate is about to befall them. Teachers
claim that 'the Department is always the one to push. Inspectors say
"If you accept these children then when we come round again we will
recommend that the school be made Coloured".' They are therefore
anxious to exclude all 'in-betweens'.

Even if the threat of reclassification as a Coloured school were a
figment of the imagination, the Principal and his teachers would still
not wish their school to become a refuge for pass-Whites, for, like
most White South Africans, they recognize the lowered status of the
Coloured people *vis-à-vis* the Whites, and many support the government policy of apartheid. Moreover, they believe that non-Whites
make inferior students, and attribute the low academic standing of the
school to the presence of Coloureds in the classroom.

As to the possibly more liberal policy of admissions among schools
of superior social standing, accommodation in such schools is in such
demand that they are free to pick and choose their pupils and, besides,
few pass-Whites can afford their fees. They need not fear being
swamped by pass-Whites. Colander High, on the other hand, has
everything to fear – its own temptation above all, for its enrolment has
declined grievously and the desire to maintain numbers tempts the
Principal to accept 'doubtful cases'.

We have seen that the Principal of Colander High School is resolved
to exclude children of swarthy complexion from his school; we have
seen the length to which he is prepared to go in giving expression to
his resolution; and we have hazarded some compelling reasons for the
existence of this resolution, which he maintains even in the face of his
personal, not illiberal, inclinations. Nevertheless, his school has the
reputation of harbouring pass-Whites, and the majority of the children
in his classrooms are in fact so dark of complexion as to raise serious
doubts as to their 'White extraction'.

This fact is commonly a subject for comment among government
officials, teachers, parents, and even the children themselves. An interview with the Departmental Psychologist revealed his preoccupation
with the complexion of children at the school – the low results obtained on the IQ tests which he administered were connected in his
mind with 'the question of colour'. School inspectors commonly broach

the topic, and indicate to teachers the children they believe to be non-White. Teachers themselves complain that 'the whole trouble with this school is that 80 to 90 per cent are Coloured', and that 'the School Board always pick on us when nobody else will accept a boy'. They ask, 'Are there any children here who are *not* Coloured?' Manifestly White residents of Colander treat the subject with some gaiety: 'Oh Lord! That's not Colander High, is it?' exclaimed one at the approach of a gang of African convicts. Among the children themselves a not uncommon term of abuse is 'kaffir'; and their friends sometimes call Colander High 'Kaffir Skool'.

There is no reliable way of determining the actual proportion of pass-Whites enrolled in the school with any accuracy; one must simply accept the evidence of one's eyes. A reliable informant with long service at the school was asked to state which of the pupils he was quite sure were White and which Coloured. Of the pupils with whom he felt sufficiently familiar in order to make such an estimate, he classified 48 per cent as White, 16 per cent as Coloured, and the remainder 'doubtful'. No clearer proof that at least some are pass-Whites can exist than the fact that down the years a number of pass-White children have been flushed out by resentful Coloured relatives. On one recent occasion a father and mother, accompanied by a very dark child, entered the Principal's office and demanded to see him. His secretary attempted to dissuade them from seeing him by announcing that an appointment would be necessary. They insisted, however, on seeing him there and then. The Principal stalled for more than half the morning until he could no longer avoid visiting his office. When he arrived they said, 'Don't worry, we are not going to ask you to take our child – we just wanted you to know that X [a boy then enrolled at the school] is a cousin of ours.' On another occasion a Coloured father, who had deserted his wife, denounced his daughter, then attending the school. 'He had to take it out on somebody,' commented a teacher. 'She was brilliant, and she wanted to raise herself. The last we heard of her she was in a non-European school.' On yet another occasion the parents of the school's Coloured handyman denounced their nephew, who had attended primary school with their son, but who was then enrolled at Colander High. These children, and many others placed in the same predicament, were expelled.[12]

How are we to account for the fact that so many children of such dark complexion are enrolled at the school in spite of the Principal's most vigorous efforts to exclude them? Some 'doubtful' children have been admitted after a successful appeal to the School Board, and there have been occasions when the Principal has been overwhelmed with pity and admitted a child against his inclinations, sometimes because the parents had attended the school, sometimes because the child had attended a White primary school.[13] None of these circumstances are, however, sufficient to account for more than a small number of dark children on the register.

We can only assume, therefore, that a large number of swarthy children have been enrolled to the school against the wishes of the Principal and at the behest of the School Committee, who, it will be remembered, are elected by parents mostly from among their own numbers. That at least some members of the School Committee seek to ensure that at least some swarthy children are admitted to the school is indicated by the fact that the Committee seldom reached a unanimous decision on the selection or rejection of a child on the grounds of colour. And it is said that Committee members have resigned over the issue 'just because it is expecting too much to make them judge over their neighbours'. Such committee members, according to one of their number, preferred to 'give the benefit of the doubt'.

The reaction of at least one former Committee member to the application of swarthy children for admission to the school has not been merely passive. Here is an eye-witness account of his efforts on behalf of pass-Whites:

> I was sitting in the home of Mr Doaks when two young women were shown in. They were sisters who had called to see him about the race classification of the younger sister. The older sister explained that her classification was 'in order' – she was classified as White. The younger sister said she had been called upon by the Population Register officials to have herself classified, but she was afraid to do so because her birth certificate described her as being of 'Mixed' birth.
>
> Mr Doaks made an uncomplimentary remark about parents who wrote 'Mixed' on birth certificates. Then he said to the younger sister: ' "Mixed" could mean "mixed" between English and Afrikaans, couldn't it?' The girls seemed relieved.
>
> Asked what school she had attended, the younger sister replied: 'Coloured'. Mr Doaks remarked: 'That does not mean you are Coloured, does it? Your parents might have sent you there because it was the nearest school.'
>
> Mr Doaks then dispatched her to an Opposition M.P., who he said would take up her case for her. He was confident of success.

Of this man pass-Whites say that 'he gets a lot of children into the schools. He tries here, he tries there, and fixes things. There was a lot of trouble with this apartheid in the schools you know. It's very difficult to get into a school. It's all a matter of influence. If one of the parents knows somebody on the Committee or a friend knows a friend, they say, "Take this child" – and it's all right.'

Finally, as evidence of the connivance of the School Committee in admitting pass-Whites to the school, there is the confession of the Principal, all the more impressive in that it was long withheld, to the effect that the exclusion of some children on the grounds of appearance 'blew them all up [the Committee, that is] because some of them were damn Coloureds. Some voted year after year: "Accept this, accept this, accept this." I wasn't going to refer a case to them if it wasn't obvious.'

The picture so far drawn of the community's connivance (through its elected School Committee) in admitting pass-Whites to the school is somewhat over-simple in that it implies a greater homogeneity of racial attitudes among residents of Colander than in fact obtains. A member of the School Committee, commenting on the exclusion of some pass-Whites from the school, said, 'What were we to do when people living right next door to the school refused to send their children there because they had heard that it accepted Coloured children and reported you to the Board who sent an Inspector round to investigate?' Those who were excluded, he said, were 'not acceptable to the community'. And just as some members of the community are more ready than others to discriminate against certain pass-Whites, so are some members of the School Committee more ready than others to discriminate. 'Most of us give the benefit of the doubt but there are always one or two who are strict.'

The picture drawn of the School Committee's actions is over-simple also in the sense that it implies that the Committee invariably acted wholly as an agent of the community. Sometimes it acted in what it perceived to be the interests of the school organization and not primarily as the community might have wished. It was the community's wish to exclude those 'not acceptable to the community', among whom were the 'obviously Coloured'. On the other hand it was in the school's interest to build up enrolment. Now how 'obvious' the 'colour' of a person is depends not only on complexion but also on the ethnic identity of relatives and known associates. Thus a person might appear 'obviously Coloured' to members of the community among whom he lives but not to strangers. So, in the words of a School Committee member, 'the policy was to accept Coloureds from outside the area but not from within'.

Colander High School then is a 'buffer school'. It has accepted pass-Whites as pupils partly because residents of Colander do not care to apply apartheid rigorously, and partly because the school Principal and the School Board often classified pupils as White or Coloured on the basis of *ad hoc* decisions. Because of decisions reached in this manner, hundreds of children of inscrutable complexion entered nominally White schools like Colander High and so were sent well on the way to successful passing for White. Some of these children were sent back to square one when their schools were reclassified as Coloured. Thus a child may be White one day and Coloured the next. All this adds point to L. G. Green's definition of a Coloured person as 'one who has failed to pass as a White'.

NOTES

1 For a brief mention of pass-White pupils in Cape Town see B. M. Kies, *The Policy of Educational Segregation and Some of its Effects Upon the Coloured People of the Cape*, unpublished thesis, University of Cape Town, 1939, p. 75. See also E. L. Maurice, *The History and Administration of the Education of the Coloured Peoples of the Cape, 1652–1910*, unpublished thesis, University of Cape Town, 1946, Vol. 2, Ch. 8.

2 As enrolment declines so does the number of teachers appointed to the school.

3 *Hansard*, col. 3419.

4 'Definition of Race: Spying, Prying, But No Finality', *Cape Argus*, 25 July 1958.

5 See *Cape School Board Annual Report*, 1956.

6 See M. Horrell, *Race Classification in South Africa – Its Effects on Human Beings*, Johannesburg, South African Institute of Race Relations, 1958, p. 16; and also, 'Sifting Children Thorny Problem, Say Principals', *Cape Times*, 7 February 1958.

7 There is good reason to believe that the actual number refused admission on the grounds of colour is in excess of twenty. Children rejected without reference to the School Committee are not included in this figure, nor are those rejected on other, ostensible, grounds. In order to forestall appeals, and the possible success of such appeals by the Board, the Principal is extremely reluctant to admit, even verbally, to the Board that a child has been refused admission on grounds of appearance.

8 See 'Race Tragedies Keep Pupils from School', *Cape Times*, 7 February 1963.

9 The anomaly has been the subject of several newspaper articles. See, for example, *Cape Times*, 7 February 1963; 8 February 1963 ('what is obvious to the eye is not always on the identity card . . .'); and *Cape Argus*, 8 February 1963.

10 'Try for White in Schools', *Cape Times*, 8 February 1963. See also, 'Star Chamber Inquisitors Weed out Colour in Cape Schools', *Cape Argus*, 29 January 1959.

11 One of the most frequent of such humiliations is the often considerable period of waiting which 'borderline' children sometimes endure while their

Chapter Five

'AD HOC-ERY'[1]

In the Introduction we asked how it could be that there still exists in the land of apartheid a number of public schools which, while reserved by law for 'Whites', nevertheless harbour a sizeable proportion of pass-Whites. Part of the answer was given in Chapter Two, which focused exclusively upon the would-be passer and on his 'White' and 'non-White' antagonists. That answer was no more than partial, a fact that became clear in the previous chapter, which took account not only of those antagonistic to passing but also to those 'Whites' who connive at it. It would seem, therefore, that in the study of upward social mobility or of assimilation it is misleading to focus on the aspirant to membership of the superordinate group, or on those who seek to deny him membership, to the exclusion of those who connive at his aspirations. The White and the would-be pass-White must be perceived as a team:

> When we allow that the individual [here, the pass-White] projects a definition of the situation when he appears before others, we must also see that the others, however passive their role may seem to be, will themselves effectively project a definition of the situation by virtue of their response to the individual and by virtue of any lines of action they initiate to him. . . .[2]

It takes two (or more) to complete the process of passing for White.

The task of the pass-White is to present himself to members of the White group in such a manner that the Whites cannot be altogether sure that he is of Coloured origin.[3] Clearly, anticipatory socialization is involved.[4] But there is more to passing than that. White persons have to decide whether or not to accept the aspirant as a member of their group. What are the grounds upon which the Whites base their decisions? The hypothesis is that the White South African who interacts with a person of not readily discernible race asks himself three questions: Is it incumbent upon me, in the circumstances, to decide whether or not this person is White? If I decide that he is White, will others go along with my estimation? And what's in it for me? That is, he acts *ad hoc* in accordance with what he perceives to be in his best interests. And according to the way he answers his own questions, so will the person of inscrutable race be classified as White or Coloured. Three illustrations are presented.

Illustration 1
A fair-skinned Coloured who lives as a Coloured and is employed as a Coloured joins, in a spirit of playfulness, the queue at a White Colander cinema. The cinema manager eyes him suspiciously, hesitates, walks away.

The cinema manager knows that if he admits Coloureds to his cinema he will be breaking the law and his customers will desert him. So, when he sees the fair-skinned Coloured in a queue, he has to reach a decision. It is not as if the Coloured person were merely asking him the time of day: in this case, and in many similar, the manager's livelihood depends on his reaching a socially acceptable decision. He decides that (a) the Coloured might be a White; (b) other Whites would not find his estimation of the Coloured's race unconvincing; and (c) to challenge the Coloured-who-might-be-a-White would cause a disturbance and a loss of custom. So he lets the man be. His decision was made *ad hoc* (that is, for the particular purpose at hand and without reference to wider application) and in accordance with his best interests as he himself perceived them.

Put another way, the cinema manager acted in accordance with what Karl Popper has called 'the logic of the situation'.[5] 'Situational logic' (or 'methodological individualism', as others have it)[6] is a heuristic device whereby the sociologist (and everyone else for that matter) endeavours to comprehend the behaviour of others by attributing to them the feelings and thoughts that he would have if he behaved in such manner[7] and by assuming that behaviour is never entirely random but that persons act more or less rationally in the light of their dispositions and understandings of their situation.[8]

When the cinema manager is faced with persons in his queue who are obviously either White or Coloured his course of action is clear – it is laid down for him in the mores of his society. When, however, the race of persons in his queue is obscure he is in a quandary as to which mores apply, and so he has recourse to *ad hoc* decisions. Once having made a number of such *ad hoc* decisions, and having observed the consequences, his decisions become less extempore and based more on experience and what might loosely be termed 'case-law'. But he cannot invariably rely upon 'case-law' to resolve his difficulty, for there are always some persons of whose race he canonot be sure, and he must either accept such persons as White or reject them as Coloured. There is no other course of action open to him. In the next case to be discussed a 'third way' was found.

Illustration 2

I once had a patient who looked White to me, though I didn't know. I got a frantic phone call from the hospital: was she a European or was she a Coloured? I said I didn't know – that's your trouble not mine. She was so dark they couldn't put her in the European ward and so fair they couldn't put her in with the Coloureds. So they put her in a side ward.

The White physician, whose surgery is in Colander, did not have to decide whether or not her patient was White. Whether or not the patient was in fact White did not affect her earnings or the legality of her ministrations. The hospital authorities did not have to reach a firm decision because the way was open for them to sidestep the issue and avoid the negative sanctions they would have incurred had they unwittingly made a wrong decision. Now let us suppose the patient was in process of passing for White, as she probably was. By virtue of the facts that she had been treated by a White physician and had occupied, unchallenged, a bed in a White hospital, albeit in a side ward, she had furthered her progress on the path of upward social mobility and of assimilation into the White group. The decisions which made this possible were made by White persons, *ad hoc*, and in the light of the best interests of physician and hospital administration as they themselves perceived them. The decisions were *ad hoc* in so far as they were made for the particular purpose at hand (accommodating the patient) and without reference to wider application (government policy, which demands total segregation of all patients by race). The dilemma with which hospital personnel were faced was not as acute as that of the cinema manager for 'case-law' indicated a 'third way' out of the dilemma – putting the patient in a side ward.

Illustration 3

As mentioned earlier, between 1932 and 1956 at least 14 White non-denominational schools under School Boards in Cape Town were reclassified as Coloured. Six of these schools were commonly known as 'buffer schools' for they admitted as pupils children described in the local School Board minutes as 'slightly Coloured' but colloquially known as 'borderline cases'. They admitted these children in the full knowledge that their actions were illegal, for the regulations had been spelled out to them by the Superintendent-General of Education as early as 1932.

The actions of school Principals in admitting 'borderline cases' to their schools can be understood in the light of decisions made in terms of the best interests of Principals as they themselves perceived them rather than in terms of the demands of apartheid. All the schools mentioned are situated in areas once predominantly White residential areas, but now predominantly Coloured. As White enrolment in these schools declined, school principals had little alternative but to admit an increasing proportion of 'borderline cases' to their schools if they wished to maintain enrolment.

The local School Board made vigorous attempts to discourage this practice by circulating warnings and by meeting with School Committees 'to impress upon them the necessity of exercising great care in admitting new children to school'. When these warnings were found to be ineffective the Board reclassified these nominally-White 'buffer schools' as Coloured, thus sticking to the letter of the law and evading the wrath of the Superintendent-General of Education.

Paradoxically, School Board officials were to some extent responsible for the very practice they were officially committed to stamp out. The primary task of the School Board was to ensure that every child under a given age and purporting to be White was placed in school. 'Borderline cases' remaining in an official's decision-pending file for any length of time (because White schools refused to accept 'borderline cases' and because the parents of these children refused to send them to Coloured schools) made him appear inefficient to his colleagues – the norms of his profession dictated that he should clear his file with dispatch. He solved this problem by sending the 'borderline cases' to nominally White 'buffer schools'. 'When these children that we tried to pretend didn't exist came to us,' said an official of the School Board, 'we said, "Why not try X School or Y School?" ' In acting thus, the official not only cleared his file but also escaped the emotional discomfort he would otherwise have suffered in face-to-face interaction with parents whose children he had relegated to Coloured status. The official thus acted *ad hoc* and in accordance with his best interests as he himself perceived them.

Not uncommonly, the School Board ordered the principals of 'buffer schools' to admit to their schools children more swarthy of complexion than the principals were willing to accept. Such Principals were willing to accept children whom they knew to be pass-Whites, but only so long as they were sufficiently fair of complexion as not to arouse the attention of White parents whose children were, or were potentially, enrolled in their schools. The School Board, on the other hand, was not concerned with the appearance of the children so

long as they were officially deemed White: the School Board's concern was with the placing of all White children in White schools.

At first blush the decisions and subsequent actions of school Principals and of the School Board appear inconsistent, even paradoxical.
Principals of 'buffer schools', anxious to maintain numbers, accept
known pass-Whites, but at the same time refuse on the grounds of
appearance children nevertheless officially deemed White. The School
Board makes vigourous attempts to curb the enrolment of pass-Whites
in nominally White schools but at the same time feeds 'buffer schools'
with 'borderline cases'. But the inconsistency is more apparent than
real and is resolved if decisions are viewed as *ad hoc* and as reached in
terms of the best interests of the school Principals and of School Board
officials as they themselves perceive them.

The number of similar cases which could be cited in support of this
thesis is legion. All concern situations in which Whites reach *ad hoc*
decisions. The significance of this must now be spelled out. When
committees are faced with an apparently intractable problem and are
deeply divided over it they as often as not resolve their difficulty by
shelving it – by appointing an *ad hoc* sub-committee. And there, perhaps, the matter rests. The White South African, faced with the difficulty of deciding upon the racial status of an aspirant pass-White
solves his problem likewise, by reaching an *ad hoc* decision; but there
the matter may not rest, for such *ad hoc* decisions may cumulatively
favour the upward mobility of the aspirant. The point to be stressed is
that while each decision is made *ad hoc*, together they constitute a
process – that process which enables some Coloured persons to change
their status to that of White persons.

The pass-White is not merely passive in the process, but actively
seeks to manipulate social norms to his advantage. He does this by
ensuring that much of his interaction with Whites is segmental.
Were a questionably White person to propose broad-based interaction
with a South African White by, for instance, requesting the hand of his
daughter in marriage, then the White man would make exhaustive
inquiries to establish the race of his prospective son-in-law. No room
here for *ad hoc* decisions: too much is at stake. Hence the hypothesis:
that aspirants to upward social mobility or to assimilation into a superordinate ethnic group gradually win acceptance by interacting segmentally with members of the superordinate group, thus allowing the
superordinate-group members leeway in which innumerable *ad hoc*
decisions cumulatively favourable to the aspirant can be made. To
bring together and sum up the words of a number of informants:

The idea is first to obtain White employment in some occupation entry to which does not require production of a [White] identity card. Government service is no good – the railways in particular – for they are strict. Tramways are excellent. Then you move to an area where some Whites live, or nearby. Then you move closer to the Whites. There's a row of houses, see. There's a vacancy and a Coloured family move in. By the time the next family moves in the first is White. Then you join White associations, especially sports clubs and churches; and you try to get your children into a White school. You cultivate White friends and encourage them to visit you. Then you get your identity card, though first you wait until you are reasonably certain that it will be White. If there is trouble then maybe you can buy one, if you know the right people in X Street.

If the pass-White is particularly acute in manipulating social norms to his advantage, he will see to it that much of his interaction with White persons is not merely segmental but also selective in that it involves formally defined roles (as between teacher and pupil, physician and patient, and so on) in which the incumbent of the superordinate role performs according to universalistic norms, treating White and pass-White alike. The words of the minister of a Colander church reveals an example of such manipulation: 'People go to church so that they can claim they are accepted as European. People come to me for certificates, and I sign them: "This is a registered European church and they attend my church." I get a bit annoyed when it's obvious, though.'9

The successful pass-White will also see to it that much of his inter-action with Whites occurs at a face-to-face level, in which case Whites are unlikely to escape embarrassment should they reach a decision adverse to the passer. Some Whites are more impervious to personal pressures than others: it has been noted that some school Principals, on taking over a school, expel pass-White children; on the other hand some Principals have resigned their posts because (they have told me) the embarrassment caused them by pass-Whites proved too much for them. Similar embarrassment has, as also previously noted, caused some members of the Colander High School Committee to resign. So effective are face-to-face pressures that in an attempt to circumvent them Whites may seek recourse to impersonal bureaucratic norms. As shown in Chapter Four, the Principal of Colander High attempted to persuade the Department of Education (the officials of which are not exposed to face-to-face interaction with passers) to deny passers access to his feeder schools, and succeeded in persuading the Western Province Land Tenure Advisory Board to zone a pre-

dominantly Coloured part of Colander for exclusive White occupation in order to reduce the number of pass-Whites applying for
admission to his school. And his satisfaction was evident when the
Population Registration Act came into force ('I can talk to them now:
"the law demands this . . ." ').

When the pass-White is near to success it is to his advantage to dis-
continue relying entirely on face-to-face pressures and to rely instead
on bureaucratic norms: when he is 'reasonably certain that it will be
White' he obtains his identity card. And, as the Colander High
Principal has been quoted as saying, 'Once they've got their cards there
is no arguing with them.' At this time it may be to the advantage of
Whites who seek to impede upward mobility of pass-Whites to
block recourse to bureaucratic norms. This is what the Principal does
when he refuses to tell the School Board that he will not, on the grounds
of colour, admit a child to his school. To confess the relevance of colour
would be to give the pass-White child the right to appeal to the School
Board and possibly to secure a bureaucratic decision in his favour.

To recapitulate, the arguments have been advanced (i) that in the
study of upward social mobility we must take account not only of
aspirants to upward social mobility and of those who seek to thwart
them, but also of those members of the superordinate group who
wittingly and unwittingly aid them; (ii) that those members of the
superordinate group who aid the aspirant to upward social mobility
commonly do so in the course of making decisions which are (a) *ad
hoc*, and (b) in accordance with the best interests of the decision-makers
as they themselves perceive them; (iii) that aspirants to upward social
mobility interact with members of the superordinate group (a) after
undergoing preliminary anticipatory socialization, (b) segmentally and
selectively, in terms of formally defined roles, and (c) initially at a
face-to-face level but subsequently in terms of bureaucratic norms,
thus creating conditions in which innumerable decisions cumulatively
favourable to the aspirant can be made by members of the superordinate group.

NOTES

1 This chapter follows closely an article by the writer, 'The Process of Passing
for White in South Africa: A Study in Cumulative Ad Hoc-ery', *Canadian Review
of Sociology and Anthropology*, Vol. 4, No. 3, pp. 14–17.

2 E. Goffman, *The Presentation of Self in Everyday Life*, New York, Doubleday,
1959, p. 9.

3 Pertinent here is Drake and Cayton's observation that 'In instances where Negroes are out of the conventional role, Whites who have stereotyped notions of what Negroes should do, where they might be found, and how they should act are led to mistake obvious Negroes for White or other racial stock' (S. C. Drake and H. R. Cayton, *Black Metropolis*, New York, Harcourt, Brace and World, 1945, p. 164). Similar observations are recounted by M. Banton in Ch. 4 of his *Race Relations*, London, Tavistock Publications, 1967, and by J. Hoetink in his *The Two Variants in Caribbean Race Relations*, London, Oxford University Press, 1967.

4 The concept is discussed by R. K. Merton in *Social Theory and Social Structure*, New York, The Free Press, 1965, Ch. 8.

5 K. Popper, *The Open Society and its Enemies*, Vol. 2. New York, Harper and Row, 1963, p. 265. See also I. Jarvie, *The Revolution in Anthropology*, New York, The Humanities Press, 1964, *passim*.

6 For example, see J. Watkins, 'Historical Explanation in the Social Sciences', in P. Gardiner (ed.) *Theories of History*, New York, The Free Press, 1964.

7 See Weber's distinction between 'explaining' and 'understanding': M. Weber, *The Theory of Social and Economic Organization*, New York, The Free Press, 1964, Ch. I (i).

8 The use of this kind of analysis appears to give rise to considerable alarm among North American sociologists. A question I am often asked is, 'Can you be sure the cinema manager did not act out of humanitarian motives?' The answer is that, while I cannot read the mind of any individual cinema manager (or even ask him, questionnaire in hand, if he is breaking the law and why), I can, as a fellow South African, 'understand' the behaviour of the 'typical manager' in so far as the behaviour is seen as social rather than psychological. Theodore Abel's well-known criticism of Weber's use of *verstehen* ('The Operation Called Verstehen', *American Journal of Sociology*, November 1948, pp. 211–18) is answered in William Tucker's 'Max Weber's Verstehen' (*The Sociological Quarterly*, Spring 1965, pp. 157–65).

9 Churches commonly patronized by pass-Whites are Lutheran, Congregational, Roman Catholic, Anglican, and Methodist. The Dutch Reformed Church in Colander has a small congregation because, they say, 'colour is so important to them'.

Chapter Six

TEACHERS AND PUPILS

Preceding chapters have dealt with the social setting of Colander High School. The remaining chapters deal with the social organization of the school and with the connection between eccentricities of the organization and the social setting. Chapters Seven and Eight are concerned with relationships between members of the teaching staff. Here we examine the relationship between teachers and pupils.

The fathers of Colander High pupils are, for the most part, skilled or semi-skilled manual workers. Their sons, in response to a questionnaire,[1] claim that they intend following in their fathers' footsteps. Almost all the boys choose occupations which fall within the skilled trades category – they want to be mechanics, fitters and turners, print compositors, electricians; most think their wishes will be realized; all believe – and in this they are encouraged by their parents – that they will in fact become tradesmen of some sort. As for the girls, there are those who wish to be air hostesses, nurses, models, or hairdressers, but most want to become – and almost all think that in fact they will become – typists or office workers of some kind. In the entire school only two children hope to pursue a professional career and neither of them expects his wishes to be realized.

The boys reject bus-conducting ('overcrowded', 'awkward hours'), and other non-trades ('Because when you've got a trade nobody can take it away from you'). By far the most numerous and vociferous hostile remarks are, however, reserved for middle-class occupations – clerk ('stuffy'), teacher ('don't like school'), doctor ('works his hole [*sic*] life threw [*sic*]'). The girls are even more class-conscious in their responses. The most commonly rejected occupations are factory hand, salesgirl and book-keeper. Their comments – 'so ordinary', 'unsuitable for any girl', 'one mixes with the wrong kind of people', 'mostly for Coloured girls'. Next in order of unpopularity come the middle-class occupations of teacher, doctor, nurse, and librarian.

Those occupations which are rejected by the children are rarely recommended to them by parents. The middle-class ones are, however, recommended by the teachers: boys who wish to be lithographers are advised to become artists, and girls who wish to be hairdressers are advised to become nurses.

The discrepancy between the goals of the children and of the teachers is emphasized by the nature of the courses offered by the school: these cater more adequately for those who wish to enter a middle-class occupation than for those who wish to acquire the specific skills of the community.

All pupils study English (seven periods a week), Afrikaans (six periods a week), and religious instruction (one or two periods a week). Other subjects studied depend on sex and stream: only girls take singing, art, domestic science, and typing, and not more than a handful take mathematics after Standard 6; only boys take carpentry and enrol as military cadets.

In Standard 6 a general course is offered.[2] Children have no option but to follow a uniform course consisting of the basic subjects – English, Afrikaans, science, mathematics, and social studies. In addition, the boys do carpentry and the girls domestic science. Physical training is taken separately by the boys and girls under two different teachers, nominally once a week. The girls have a practical art lesson, the boys a lecture from an itinerant teacher once a week. To make up for this, the boys have two religious instruction periods per week while the girls have but one. Out of the 40 periods per week, 13 are devoted to languages, 12 to mathematics and science, 6 to social studies, 6 to religious instruction, physical training, singing, and art, and only 3 to the specifically vocational domestic science and carpentry.

In Standard 7 the children are shunted into three streams: Commercial Girls, Commercial Boys, and Technical Boys. All devote the same amount of time to languages and the sciences, social studies, and religious instruction. Domestic science, carpentry, art, and singing are dropped – in some cases temporarily. The Commercial girls do book-keeping, business methods, and typing; the Commercial boys book-keeping, business methods, and mathematics; the Technical boys commercial arithmetic, mathematics, science, and metalwork. Of the forty periods per week only six are devoted to specifically vocational subjects.

The Lynds' wry comment on schooling in Middletown applies with equal force to schooling in Colander:

Square root, algebra, French, the battles of the civil war . . . the ability to write composition or to use semicolons, sonnets, free verse, and the Victorian novel – all these and many other things that constitute the core of education simply do not operate in life as Middletown adults live it.[3]

The teaching of any vocational skills at all, it is true, represents a compromise on the part of the teachers. And it is a compromise which cannot be said to have their wholehearted support: teachers find most satisfaction in teaching the 'classier' subjects; and those who rank lowest in the staff-room (apart from those whose appointment is temporary) are those who teach manual or vocational subjects. But, from the point of view of the parents, it is not a sufficient compromise: 'Why must my children learn subjects which will be no use to them?' they demand.

Teachers do not of course confine their teaching to what is formally laid down in the curriculum or to technical matters, to skills designed to make pupils useful and productive. They are also concerned with what has been called 'regulatory' teaching – teaching designed to regulate pupils' behaviour in social intercourse. Thus, they extol the virtues of 'patriotism, of loyalty, or obedience to one's superiors and to God'. They applaud 'dignity of effort and sacrifice'. Their Principal announces that 'We strive to create that spirit in the school that will make it easier for our scholars to choose the way of upright, decent, honest living.' These are values and attitudes which the English Public School boy accepts almost as part of the topography and as so obviously right that it is hardly worth discussing them. But they do not strike a sympathetic chord in the minds of residents of Colander.

Parents and teachers disagree about the kind of social behaviour that is permissible in children. Pupils are expelled for what appear to parents as trivial offences – for 'parading in the street at night, all dolled up, smoking and swearing and using obscene language in the company of a low type of fellow'. A mother recounts:

Last year Georgie phoned me up at work to say that the Vice-Principal wouldn't let him write his exams because he came without a tie – I wasn't there in the morning to see – so I phoned him up. It must have been one of his off days. He was sarcastic and I played up to him. I said if he didn't let Georgie write I'd go to the Board. So he came down in his car to fetch him and he found him in front of the wireless smoking. He phoned me up and said, 'You know where I found him?' I said he'd be at home. He said, 'But do you know what he was doing?' I said, 'Probably smoking.' He said, 'Exactly'. (I let the two elder boys smoke at home, but they know never to take their cigarettes to school. And they mustn't smoke in front of visitors, even if their tongues are hanging out for a cigarette.) So he took him down to the Principal and lectured him and said he was a bad boy.

Disagreement is particularly strong between parents and teachers concerning the goals of education. The school Principal writes, 'In preparing our scholars for life, we consider that the development of character and the recognition of spiritual values are of as much importance as the acquiring of factual knowledge.' This is a sentiment he has hammered home in speeches made at prizegiving ceremonies down the years: 'There are those,' he says,

> who think education is but a training for some particular function in society – to become an engine driver or a book-keeper or a shop-assistant . . . but the acquiring of factual knowledge and manual skills does not of itself make a good man or a bad man . . . but if it is coupled with a sense of spiritual responsibility and a high purpose in life, we have true education. . . .

Education is an attitude of mind', pontificates the school magazine, 'and it does not consist in a quantum of knowledge. It is that attitude of mind that will send a boy or girl into life filled with the love and self-sacrifice that was taught here on earth by Jesus of Nazareth, filled with the eager curiosity and love of balance and beauty of the Greek, filled with the stability and love of country of the best of the Romans.' Parents, on the other hand – invariably in my experience – see their children's schooling in the light of how it affects their potential earning capacity. Employers are demanding higher academic qualifications from employees than they used to: that is why parents want their children 'to realize how important education is nowadays'. 'Times are bad,' parents complain, 'even with a Standard 8 you must tramp the streets for a job.' Fathers of meagre schooling find themselves in uncongenial employment: their sons must do better: 'If you haven't education, you're nothing – I want my children to be higher than I am, not lower.' But daughters do not matter so much. 'She'll need a Standard 8 for her job, but it's not for me to tell her to go any higher if she doesn't want to.' After all, 'The girl is going to get married, so why worry?' And besides, girls have to learn how to keep house: 'It's not like a boy – she's got to learn to be at home.'

It might be thought that parents who are anxious that their children pass for White and be upwardly mobile would not jib at the children's acquiring the middle-class values which teachers seek to impress upon them. A dark-complexioned father, a bus conductor, who wanted his son 'to go as far as possible' in school, who desired that his son should not remain 'low like me', and who thought it the duty of teachers 'to rise [sic] my son', seemed, when I first encountered him, to support such an argument. However, upon further inquiry I discovered that he wanted his son to enter a trade and that by 'as far as possible' he meant 'until he reaches minimum school-leaving age'. The goals which parents and teachers have in mind for the children do not coincide.

Teachers and parents disagree not only about the purposes of schooling but also about the techniques whereby these purposes are to be achieved. The sanctions employed by parents on their children strike the teachers as a mixture of the savage and the permissive, while the sanctions employed by the teachers often strike the parents as derisory. Teachers regard their pupils as moral agents. They use words like 'deserve', 'justice', 'honour', and 'misconduct'. They appeal to children to behave 'like gentlemen', and demand evidence of 'team spirit'. In other words they expect children to internalize middle-class values. Parents have few such expectations. The punishment they administer consists largely of frequent thrashings and vociferous scoldings. Children soon learn, many of them, to regret, not the misdemeanour, but being caught at it; and a scolding is as water off a duck's back. So the Principal of Colander High is left to lament ineffectually that 'Parents know naught of psychology and have had little, if any, training in rearing and caring for children.'[4]

With teachers and parents at loggerheads in such crucial matters as the goals of education, and the means whereby these are to be achieved, it is inevitable that the war that pupils wage upon their teachers is tinged with deep-seated animosity, an animosity no better evidenced than in the type of leader that the class throws up. These are the toughs and repeaters (those who are repeating a year's work because they failed on their first attempt). In one junior class of 27, in which an election for the class captain was held, the 8 repeaters between them got 120 votes, and the 19 who were not repeaters got 48. There comes to mind Blau and Scott's observation that

> in groups organized in outright opposition to the formal organization, such as are found in prisons or concentration camps, high informal status probably accrues to those members who can most effectively resist organizational pressures; that is, to the 'low producers' from the standpoint of the formal organization.[5]

How does animosity between teachers and pupils affect the social organization of the school? It is instructive at this point to compare the social organization of Colander High with that of the English Public School.

The social organization of an English Public School[6] is in some respects analogous to that of primitive tribes with a segmentary political structure (such as the Nuer of the Southern Sudan)[7] in that individuals and groups unite in opposition to and in competition with structural equivalents, form against form, school class against school class, and sex against sex. Cross-cutting loyalties prevent the emergence of a cleavage along one axis, and so help to maintain the cohesion of the group. Forms and classes are cemented by their members' cross-cutting allegiances to school houses, clubs, and societies – and by an allegiance to the school as a whole, fostered by the flourishing of school insignia, by the ritual and ceremonial attendant upon morning assembly, and by competition with other schools on the sports field.

Teachers predetermine the membership and formal organization of the school, create the forces which weld the pupils together, and manipulate mechanisms whereby they are subdivided. They do so to suit their own ends. By creating a structure of classes and forms, of clubs and societies, of prefects, class captains and underlings, of groups based on sex and on age, they pit child against child and obviate the emergence of a phalanxed body of children sustained by consentaneous loyalties. Only teachers stand united and undivided. And by promoting at school assemblies, through homily and prayer, sentiments of solidarity embracing children and adults alike, they perpetuate their despotic power. Herein lies the genius of school organization.

Forms, clubs, and societies, streams and school houses, all, in some measure, define themselves in and are sustained by rivalry with structural equivalents: only the class normally draws much of its strength from opposition to teachers. Never does a class act with such *esprit de corps* or with such unity of purpose as when it brings a timorous and irresolute teacher to bay and closes in for the kill. Thus of all the groups in the school the class is, from the point of view of the teachers, the most dangerous. Classes are normally at war with their teachers, even in the most renowned of schools – no one who has read *The Loom of Youth*[8] or who has himself plotted with his classmates to discomfit a teacher can doubt that – but at Colander High this war is, as will be argued, fought with a boldness nourished by singularly unadulterated allegiances and with a ferocity sharpened by conflicts whose sources lie beyond the classroom.

The pre-eminence of the class as a unit of social structure at Colander High – and the extraordinary threat which it presents to the authority of teachers – is in part a consequence of the unconsolidated nature of, and even the absence of, other groups at Colander High which might compete for the class members' allegiance: there are, as we shall see, no school houses and few sports clubs and societies; social categories

based upon sex and standard-membership lack cohesion; and there is
little to divert a class member's loyalty from his class to the school as
a whole. In these ways Colander High differs from English Public
Schools.

Standards at Colander High are hierarchically ordered and numbered.
Each is primarily an administrative unit whose personnel are selected
by teachers in such a way that they are relatively homogeneous in
terms of age and academic achievement. A child enters the school at
the age of about thirteen and is enrolled in Standard 6, and normally
leaves three or four years later when he finishes Standard 8 or reaches
the age of sixteen. At the end of each year, provided teachers think his
academic progress warrants it, he is moved with his fellows to a superior
standard until he eventually leaves school altogether.

Standards are social units in terms of a shared designation, and in
terms of a nebulous fellow-feeling which stems from a certain similarity
of age and academic achievement, and from the fact that in some
circumstances teachers treat them as social units. But standards are not
social groups – they are social categories, the members of which rarely
act in concert except at the instigation of teachers or in defence of
their collective status, as when a play-group composed of members of a
senior standard turn upon a junior who wishes to join them. Even this
last reaction is uncommon at Colander High, for there are so many
academic repeaters in the school, so many children aged 15 or 16 in
Standard 6. Children of high status in terms of standard-membership
are reluctant to spurn children who, though of a junior standard, rank
high in terms of the principle of age.

But however lacking in cohesion forms may be, they are, in English
Public Schools, manipulated in such a way as to enhance the power of
teachers, for they are encouraged to compete with each other towards
common goals set by teachers. In competing with each other *qua*
form members on the playing field or in fund-raising, children in a
Public School acquire a loyalty wider than that of the classroom, and,
while they are divided in competition, the teachers stand united.
Divide et impera. This strategy is rarely employed in relation to standard-membership by Colander High teachers, for its employment
focuses children's attention upon standard-membership; and this the
Colander High teachers seek to avoid. The reason is that the senior
standards – those which rank highest in the esteem of children – are
the standards that present the greatest threat to the authority of teachers.
A considerable proportion of senior standard-membership is made up
of repeaters, and repeaters, soured by their lack of academic success,

and irked by the prolongation of their social adolescence, feel that they have little stake in the school system and so become rebels, continually sniping at teachers' authority.

It is significant that the younger children in the school are the ones whose judgement of their peers (as revealed in essays) is most closely in accord with that of their teachers, and that the older the children, the more teachers' and pupils' evaluations diverge, and the more the attitude of children to teachers becomes tinged with cynicism and hostility. The younger children write, in school essays, that the kind of children teachers like best are well-behaved, obedient and quiet, and that teachers are particularly pleased by silence, attention, obedience, and politeness. The older children, on the other hand, think that teachers like (in this order) 'goodies', 'squares', and those who are 'intelligent', 'wealthy', 'well-mannered', 'neat', and 'quiet'. Nothing makes them quite so pleased as 'creeping' ('Yes Sir, No Sir, Can I do this for Sir, Can I do that for Sir?') and, to a lesser extent, 'laughing at their jokes', 'giving them sweets', 'keeping quiet', and 'doing as you are told', and – lastly, 'working'. The younger children say that they look up to those 'who work hard', are 'quiet and well-behaved', to those who, as they report, teachers make prefects and class captains, or who are entrusted with chores such as making teachers' tea or cleaning the blackboard. They claim to like those who 'set a good example', 'do a lot for the school', and 'give the school a good name'. They dislike 'bullies' and those who 'smoke and swear'. The older boys, in contrast, more often than not, single out for attack prefects, class captains, 'teachers' pets', and 'bullies'; and they wax caustic at the expense of 'creepers', 'hangers-on', 'ratters', 'nickers', 'squirts', and 'moffies' (sissies).

The older pupils of Colander High rebel because they see the school as less and less rewarding and meaningful, less and less relevant to work and home. They pass many social landmarks while still at school – the first pair of long trousers, the first drink and cigarette, and often the first job and girl-friend – and their status as schoolchildren is not in accord with their near adult status outside the school. Sniffing the approach of emancipation from the tyranny of school, they champ at the bit provocatively. In one recent year all the prefects were suspended from office because they had as a group dismantled a car standing near the school grounds and sold it for scrap iron. Thus, the older pupils, instead of being the most amenable group to teachers are the most intractable and are, from the teachers' point of view, an undesirable group for juniors to model themselves on. The contrast with English

Public Schools, in which seniors may be a most valuable means of socializing their juniors in a direction desired by teachers,[9] is marked, as is the contrast between the teacher-authorized powers of Public School seniors and those of Colander High. No Colander High graduate could ever reminisce about his old school in the same vein as Cyril Connolly does about his:

> In practice Eton was not a democracy for the system was feudal. The masters represented the church, with the headmaster as Pope; the boys, with their hierarchy of colours and distinctions, were the rest of the population, while the prefects and athletes, the captains of houses and the members of 'Pop' were the feudal overlords who punished offences at the request of the 'church' and in return were tacitly allowed to break the same rules themselves. Thus a boy had two loyalties, to his tutor and to his fagmaster or feudal overlord.[10]

Standards are cut vertically by divisions based on sex. Half the classes in Colander High are single-sex and, in the others, boys and girls sit on different sides of the room. The sexes use different staircases, different sections of the playground, enter morning assembly from different sides of the hall, and follow different curricula. Whereas the girls study cooking, art, and singing, and play tennis, the boys study carpentry, do military cadets, and play rugby football. The division between the sexes is profound.

Sexual segregation among the children of Colander High is all the more profound for being in accord with the values of the community and of the teachers. The community is characterized by a marked polarization of the sexes. After marriage, husbands and wives generally spend little of their leisure hours in each other's company, unless, as is becoming increasingly common, they are able to afford a car and can go out together over the weekend: more usually, men go to soccer or to the pub while women visit their relatives or stay at home and listen to commercial radio. Teachers discourage interaction between the sexes lest girls fall pregnant and the school acquires a 'bad name'. They sharply reprimand girls who seek to enhance their femininity by wearing make-up or jewellery and any unseemly behaviour is the inspiration for a sermon on 'Purity' at morning assembly.

The division between the sexes, like the division between standards, is not very useful from the point of view of teachers seeking to divide and rule, for the division is virtually ineffectual in promoting competition among children. The disparity of roles between children of different sexes is so great that there are few activities in which boys and girls are ready to compete against each other. For one thing, they cannot compete with each other in the many spheres in which society allocates to them different activities: the girls cannot emulate the boys at cadets, rugby football, or carpentry and the boys cannot rival the girls at tennis or domestic science. Further, subtle but pervasive expectations discourage competition between the sexes for the favour of teachers and for academic kudos. Girls are expected to be 'well-behaved', relatively studious, and to take their work fairly seriously, while it is little disgrace for a boy to be near the bottom of his class; the well-behaved and obtrusively studious boy is rejected by his peers as a 'sissy'. Girls primly censure 'sloppy ducktail types' who 'drink, use foul language and keep bad company', while boys reserve their most caustic comments for 'creepers', 'squirts', and 'moffies'.

Standards are subdivided into classes. These are carved out by adults on the basis of sex and academic performance and are functionally related to teaching requirements. It is convenient that children of roughly the same academic ability and who follow the same curriculum should be grouped together.

Classes constitute the most closely knit social groups among the children of Colander High. Members of the same class, except where a class contains both boys and girls, follow the same curriculum and spend their working-days in the same rooms being taught by the same teachers. They, more than any other group in the school, have the most opportunity for continual and lengthy interaction. In consequence, classes form the basis for the membership of most informal groups, clubs, and societies; and even on the sports field members of the same class tend to choose each other as fellow team-members.

The cohesion of the class, resting upon the foundation of intense and prolonged interaction, and evidenced by the solidarity which class members are capable of displaying with or against particular teachers (no schoolboy crime is more heinous than informing on his fellows) is buttressed by an opposition between classes (which is more intense and more readily expressed than that which obtains between forms); by competition among individuals striving towards common goals within each class; by the existence of a formal structure of class captain, vice-captain, and followers – a structure which has the blessing of the adults and which has no equivalent at the standard level. It is shored up by the coincidence in one group of equivalence of standard, academic and sporting skill, and, to an extent, of age and sex.

The relative prominence of the class as a unit of social structure is one of the most remarkable ways in which Colander High differs from the Public School. In such schools not only are groups other than classes sturdier (forms, for example, may interact at table and in chapel) but they exhibit a greater diversity: there are groups such as those based on membership of dormitories, which do not exist at Colander High, and there is a profusion of clubs and societies.

Nowhere is the drama of school life enacted with greater fervour than in the boarding House of the English Public School. Nowhere more than in the House is competition so passionate, opposition to structural equivalents so lusty, loyalty so infectious. Nowhere more than in the House is the reward for conformity to group expectation more evident, the price of rebellion more terrible, or the subjugation of the individual to the group more complete. These Houses – probably the most potent tools for socializing children and for structuring relations among them that are available to teachers – do not exist at Colander High.[11] There did once exist, however, mere shadows of such institutions, also known as Houses, which consisted of groups of children sharing a common title and colours who competed against each other in various activities. Their function was primarily to promote rivalry at athletics: but the people of Colander play plebeian soccer and care little for athletics, so athletics faded away, and with them, the Houses.

Other groups of the kind which, while a function of the school situation are not a necessary corollary of it, are clubs, societies, and sports teams. In the English Public School these are numerous and are patronized by pupils and teachers alike. They contribute significantly to the cohesion of the entire school, for they cut across divisions based on age and bring together teachers and pupils and children of different classes and forms. They provide opportunity for competition, constitute a focus for group loyalties, and afford the individual satisfactions (and a stake in the system) which he might not find elsewhere.

What clubs exist at Colander High? Putting the best face forward, the Principal reported to the Department of Education in a recent year that 30 boys played cricket, 30 hockey, 18 rugby football, and that 24 girls played tennis, 25 hockey, 30 netball, and 8 badminton. Even these dismal figures are suspect, for games are seasonal and often fitfully organized, team membership is often duplicated and frequently merely nominal. What of societies? There is but one, the Christian League, which, with a mere handful of adherents, meets once a week for half an hour before school. There are no youth movements, no debating society, and the dramatic society's last production took place some years ago.

The reasons for the dearth of teacher-sponsored extra-curricular activities at Colander High are complex and ramified, but two might be conveniently made explicit now. First, the extra-curricular activities which receive the willing support of teachers are not often those in which residents of Colander engage spontaneously. Secondly, just as nothing succeeds like success, so nothing fails like failure: success on the games field begets further successes, while continued failure is enervating to team spirit and to the desire to continue playing.

The pursuits of Colander's adults and adolescents are not those of the teachers, or those around which teachers care to construct a network of clubs and societies. Adolescents of school-going age roam around the streets if parents are out working, and sometimes even when they are not; otherwise they entertain their friends at home, or meet them at the cinema or the church guild. They, like their parents, generally belong to no voluntary associations other than churches – there is hardly a Boy Scout or Girl Guide in the school.[12] And also like their parents, there are few of them who participate enthusiastically in organized sports, though spectator sports – soccer and baseball especially – have their devotees, and there are a handful of boys in the school who play soccer or baseball for outside clubs (for these sports are not played in the school). Such leisure pursuits have little in common with those once organized at the school by the teachers. The school magazine records the birth – and death – of a play-reading circle, a science club, an Eisteddfod, regular musical concerts, tennequoits, shooting, athletics, table tennis, and soccer.

Soccer died not for want of the support of children (before the Second World War the school fielded two teams which on several occasions held the shield) but because the Principal wanted his boys to play rugby football so that they might associate on the playing fields with 'the better schools'. Yet the sporting association of Colander High with 'the better schools' is slender. While no account of the social or academic standing of White schools is taken in the drawing-up of team fixtures, circumstances conspire to keep interaction between Colander High and 'the better schools' down to a minimum. For one thing, Colander High is usually knocked out of the competition at an early stage, and return matches are commonly played only among 'the better schools'. These schools, being wealthy, have the playing fields on which pupils may practice – while there is not a single playing field among all the schools in Colander. The pupils of these schools also have the time in which to practise and to play more games, for a proportion of them are boarders: they participate not only in the 'open' fixtures but also in privately arranged and exclusive tourneys among themselves. Their boys look sturdier, healthier, and better fed than those of Colander. And they are able to field many more teams than

Colander High, for the number of their pupils is larger, the proportion of older pupils is higher, and support for rugby football much keener.

Once a school finds itself consistently at the bottom of the league, as does Colander High, circumstances conspire to keep it there. Games masters of the 'better schools', knowing that their matches with Colander High are 'unimportant', cancel the matches for capricious reasons (and, some masters bitterly allege, for 'snobbish' reasons). Should a match take place, the Colander High team is not unlikely to be barracked by a hostile audience taunting them with the derisory epithet 'Kaffir Skool!' The players lose heart and fail to attend practices or even, sometimes, the matches themselves.

We have said that at Colander High the class is an unusually prominent unit of social structure, and we have claimed that one of the reasons for this is that there are no other groups in the school – no Houses, standards, clubs, societies, or sex groupings – which can compete with the class for the child's loyalties. We can now add that not even the school itself diverts a child's first allegiance from his class.

In the English Public School the social structure of the children is not only well articulated but also well integrated: there exists throughout the school a fellow-feeling which overrides all rivalries and antagonisms, is emblazoned in uniforms, crests, songs, and mottoes, dramatized at morning assembly, brandished in the face of outsiders, intensified in competition with other schools, and receives its ultimate expression in the mobilization of individual attitudes and endeavours to group objectives. Like such a school, Colander High has its uniforms and other insignia; not, it is true, hallowed by age or sanctified by tradition – and the crest is of hardboard, not of a patinaed bronze or weather-beaten marble – but, nevertheless, adequate. And it has its regular morning assembly: the children troop in, the youngsters first, the prefects last, the boys on one side, the girls on the other; facing their assembled teachers they stand, chorus a perfunctory 'Good Morning!', mumble their way through the Lord's Prayer (hymns are too rowdy, and are not sung), listen disconsolately while their Principal invokes the time-worn shibboleths, denounces sin, exhorts 'The Right Attitude', pronounces sentence on culprits unlucky enough – or foolish enough – to be apprehended: thus is the structure of the school enacted in ritual and consecrated in the *obiter dicta* of the Principal. Like an English Public School, Colander High preens itself self-consciously on speech days: on these occasions everyone is conscious of an identity held in common – the girls will not snicker or the boys leave their hair unbrushed lest the 'Good Name' of the school be tarnished or mother ashamed of her child: but, alas, such days are infrequent – one a year, in fact – and they lack the social glitter, the pomp and circumstance, of the renowned school's Open Day and Old Boys' Dinner. Like such a school, too, it competes with others on the sports field, but, as we have seen, such competition is desultory, half-hearted, and is a flux too torpid and uninspiring to weld the school together. And, finally, like such a school, it fosters team games (not, we repeat, with much success) that the individual may feel fully incorporated into the school, and it attempts to give individualistic performances a collective orientation (as in games where points were allotted to Houses as a whole). But the muezzin's cry of 'Team Spirit' and 'Good Name of the School' is faint. The contrast with schools which, like the English Public Schools, succeed in 'making the individual value himself only as part of the group and as part of an historical continuum',[13] and which are patronized by families generation after generation, is poignant. Not more than a handful of Colander High children know which school their mothers or fathers attended.

The Public School shibboleths have been usurped by a kind of Christianity, which the Principal finds a panacea for all kinds of school's ills. Appeals for 'Team Spirit' are made in religious terms: 'There is one God, one Father, and He is in all of us: Let us discipline ourselves; Let us pull together, help each other fight evil; Let us learn the right values.' Children are led in prayer for those who have been expelled, and for newly appointed prefects, who stand, blushing, at the back of the hall. Staff meetings and morning assemblies open with a prayer. The success of the school, as gauged by the Principal in his reports to the Department, is estimated in terms of the number of children who have 'found God'.

'X is a cripple,' writes the Principal,

> . . . who, through the help of the staff has come into a deeper Christian experience. Her mental ability is slightly below average. . . . Her home environment leaves much to be desired, as can be seen from her personal appearance. . . . Through her faith at recent healing services conducted by Mrs. Y – she went on my recommendation – her back and side have been strengthened marvellously and the doctor at the hospital told her the change was remarkable. This girl is bearing a fine Christian witness in the school and even though she obtain a mere minimum of marks, I classify her as another of God's successes.

But such religiosity cannot be described as an effective bond between the members of the school, for it is not shared by the majority of the staff ('These bloomin' speeches make me feel as if everything I do is a sin') and it is regarded by most parents and children as bizarre, and, by some, as contemptible. Said a mother:

> The Principal does it in a roundabout and soft way. A few years ago when I was working I was late one morning and my daughter thought I was gone. I went to the back and found her smoking. I gave her such a hiding, you know – I was late, but I made myself later: as a matter of fact that's how she's got two front teeth missing today. So she went to the Principal and said her mother was nasty and she was going to run away from home. So he preached to her and I don't know what he said, but he said she mustn't run away unless she took her Bible and she was first to go home and read it. So she came home and read her Bible and she didn't run away. Well, that's one way of doing things. He'd rather preach than cane.

So neither the school, nor any unit of social structure in the school – except the class – functions effectively as a focus of loyalties for the pupils of Colander High. And, as we have already noted, the class is, from the point of view of the teachers, the most dangerous unit, for more than any other unit of social structure in the school it draws its strength from opposition to teachers. And this opposition, normal to class–teacher relationships, is at Colander High sharpened by conflicts whose sources lie beyond the classroom. Pupils, resentful of attempts to make them conform to middle-class modes of behaviour, bored by the seeming irrelevance to their lives of a curriculum with a middle-class bias, fight, like the 'Young Devils' described by John Townsend,[14] and like the pupils of John Webb's 'Black School'[15] a 'guerrilla war to be [themselves] by being spontaneous, irrepressible and rule breaking'.

This friction between teachers and pupils feeds upon itself. A teacher cannot afford to allow ever-present hostility to break out into classroom disorder by permitting the expression of spontaneity and independence: his technique of control is therefore confined to drilling, to the teaching of mechanical skills, to the maintenance of rigid standards of conduct: these maintain hostility and therefore the need for further drilling.[16]

But however sharp the hostility, teachers do not go in fear of physical assault as they do in the novel *Blackboard Jungle*.[17] The relative benignity of teacher–pupil relations may be accounted for in terms of selective recruitment, in terms of the possible existence of cross-cutting allegiances of a kind not elicited in this study, and in terms of the fear of expulsion. The Principal says that there are in the school 'some boys and girls who troop in and out of the juvenile courts'; but most 'roffs' are screened out in the selection process. Attempts at inducing pupils to talk freely about their informal social organization failed, leaving open the possibility that allegiances at an informal peer-group level cross-cut pupils' allegiances to their classes, induce wider loyalties, and take some of the force out of teacher–class conflict. The explanation which teachers favour, however, is that pass-White children feel it a privilege to be in a White school and take care not to jeopardize that privilege by tormenting their teachers beyond endurance. This suggests that a group characterized by a marked cleavage (even one as marked as that portrayed here) and by few or no cross-cutting allegiances may be viable provided group members perceive a sufficiently great need to retain their membership.

The relationship between the teachers and pupils of Colander High is not a happy one, and this partly accounts for the rapid turnover of recruits to the teaching staff, the consequence of which is examined in the next chapter.

NOTES

1 See Appendix B.

2 The South African *standard* is the analogue of the British *form* and the American *grade*. The high school extends over five standards, numbered 6 to 10. The pupil is promoted from one standard to the next at the end of each school year provided that examination results justify promotion.

Standards are subdivided into classes (of perhaps thirty pupils each), on the basis of academic performance and sex.

3 R. S. and H. M. Lynd, *Middletown*, New York, Harcourt, Brace and World, 1929, p. 221.

4 For a comparison of the different child-training techniques found among slum families and families which send their children to Public Schools in England see B. M. Spinley, *The Deprived and the Privileged*, London, Routledge and Kegan Paul, 1953.

5 P. M. Blau and W. R. Scott, *Formal Organizations*, San Francisco, Chandler Publishing Co., 1962, p. 95.

6 For an account of English Public Schools see, for example, J. Wilson, *Public Schools and Private Practice*, London, Allen and Unwin, 1962, or R. Wilkinson, *The Prefects*, London, Oxford University Press, 1964.

7 For an analysis of the Nuer in the light of conflict theory see M. Gluckman, *Custom and Conflict in Africa*, Oxford, Basil Blackwell, 1960, Ch. I.

8 A. Waugh, *The Loom of Youth*, London, Grant Richards, 1918.

9 E. Bowen, in G. Greene (ed.), *The Old School*, London, Jonathan Cape, 1934, pp. 53–4, describes a neat example of such socialization: 'The first day of term seven seniors shut themselves up and, by rotative bidding, each picked up from the rest of the school a team of about eight for table at meals. Each team

moved round each week to the next seven dining-room tables, each table presided over by one of the staff. The object of each team was to make the most conversation possible, and to be a success. . . . The great thing was to amuse the mistress whose table it was, and to keep her smiling constantly. . . . Many of us have grown up to be good hostesses.'

10 C. Connolly, *Enemies of Promise*, London, Routledge and Kegan Paul, 1949, p. 179.

11 The power of the boarding-school House as a socializing agency is indicated by J. D. Pringle in 'The British Commune', published in *Encounter*, Vol. 26, No. 2, 1961, pp. 24–8 and by I. Weinberg in *The English Public Schools*, New York, Atherton Press, 1967.

12 There is a great deal of evidence to support the contention that the lower the class position the lower the rate of voluntary association membership. See, for example, M. Hausknecht, *The Joiners*, New York, The Bedminster Press, 1962.

13 R. Wilkinson, *op. cit.*, p. 42.

14 J. Townsend, *The Young Devils*, London, Chatto and Windus, 1958.

15 J. Webb, 'The Sociology of a School', *British Journal of Sociology*, Vol. 13, No. 3, 1962, pp. 264–72.

16 The point is made by J. Webb, *ibid.*

17 E. Hunter, *Blackboard Jungle*, New York, Simon and Schuster, 1954.

Chapter Seven

LONG-TERM TEACHERS
AND RECRUITS

The relationship between the teachers and pupils of Colander High has been described, as have the reciprocal effects of this relationship and the formal organization of the children. In the following two chapters we turn our attention to intra-staff relationships.

The social structure of the staff-room can be seen as a system of defences against intruders, against representatives of the State or of the family, who would trespass upon areas in which teachers believe that they alone have the competence and the right to exercise authority. The teaching staff is, as Waller has it, 'a fighting group'.[1] To defend itself it organizes and conspires: hierarchism and solidarity are its salient characteristics.

The hierarchism of the staff of Colander High is, in some ways, eccentric. At any one time the teachers of Colander High can be divided into two broad categories: those who have joined the school as a temporary expedient and who in all probability will shortly leave for other schools, and those who came to the school either out of choice or expediency and who have remained for some years. These two groups we might call the tiros and the long-term teachers, and the cleavage between them runs deeper than any other among the staff. Other eccentricities of structure are also in evidence: the Principal is unable to exert his legitimate powers to the full; the Vice-Principal and the caretaker are vested with extraordinary authority; the Principal is locked in combat with his Vice-Principal, and the Vice-Principal with the caretaker. The solidarity of the Colander High staff is also, in one respect, eccentric: tiros honour it more in the breach than in the observance.

These eccentricities can be related, on the one hand, to the scarcity of teachers and to teachers' aspiration to teach at 'good' schools, and, on the other hand, to Colander High's 'bad name' – a function partly of the 'undesirable' scholars which the school recruits and partly of the school's inimical relations with parents and bureaucrats.

This chapter deals with the notion of solidarity and the cleavage between long-term teachers and tiros. The succeeding chapter deals with hierarchism.

In industrialized societies a school finds itself caught between the conflicting particularistic demands of the family and the universalistic demands of the State. The school teachers' position would be intolerable were not the conflicting pressures exerted upon them to some extent cushioned by the intervention of School Committees, School Boards, and Parent–Teacher Associations. But such bodies cannot shield teachers from all pressures exerted upon them: bureaucrats and individual parents can and do intervene directly in the affairs of the school; moreover, School Boards and Committees, being in possession of a degree of autonomy, themselves exert pressures on teachers. Teachers have to contend also with the Trojan horse of rebellious youth, whose mutinous proclivity might at any time be boosted to a dangerous degree by the abetment of parents. But teachers too are in possession of a degree of autonomy. They are entrusted by the family and the State with the education of youth and they have their own ideas about how this mandate is to be interpreted and about how it is to be effected. They see themselves as exercising expertise in an area in which they alone have special competence and they resent what they perceive as unwarranted intrusions upon their business by the State or the family. The structure of staff-room relationships can be seen as partly a response to this situation.

The threat of parental or State interference is one which every teaching staff must meet and all respond to with solidarity, but the nature or degree of solidarity varies from school to school. The social structure of the staff of Colander High is marked by certain eccentricities: a division between long-term teachers and tiros is fundamental; and there are times when the tiros crack wide open the wall of solidarity by disparaging their colleagues in the presence of outsiders. The argument pursued in this chapter is that this eccentricity is a function of the local social context.

Discussions with teachers indicate that to them a popular school is one which, to put the matter crudely, is prestigious and has harmonious intra-staff relations. Teachers feel that the glory of such a school is reflected on to them, so they compete with each other to join its staff. Popular schools are thus in a position to pick and choose their recruits. Colander High School is not a popular school, and so, while the chronic shortage of teachers obtains,[2] it is unable to attract a fair quota of recruits.

Colander High is perhaps the least popular White school in Cape Town for it is situated in what is, by White middle-class standards, a run-down area and it attracts pupils with whom teachers would rather not be associated. They are either pass-Whites or form the poorest section of the White population. Many speak English with a traceable Afrikaans accent. The scores they obtain on IQ tests are dismal. According to the group test taken by the Departmental Psychologist in two recent years, there was not one pupil in the youngest class with an IQ above normal. Of the 177 pupils tested, 111 had an IQ of less than 88 ('dull normal'); 25 were below 75 ('mentally retarded'); and some were as low as 55.[3] The low scores obtained on IQ tests are paralleled by poor academic results: about one out of four takes the normal three years to pass from Standard Six to Standard Eight. Some parents claim that they are ashamed to tell people that their children attend the school and that 'as soon as employers hear the name of Colander High they seem to change their minds'. Not unnaturally, enrolment has declined (by 40 per cent between 1940 and 1960), the school has been subject to unofficial boycott by its feeder schools, and it has had to recruit, in the words of the Principal, 'what others do not want'.

For a teacher to accept a post at Colander High is to attract scorn from his colleagues and to invite consternation among his friends and relations, so few come to the school out of choice.[4] Even fewer remain out of choice, because a teacher who remains at the school for more than a year or so jeopardizes his career: he compromises his reputation as a 'good' teacher.

From informal conversations among teachers in Cape Town it can be inferred that to them being a 'good' teacher means possessing the ability to maintain classroom order, having the knack of producing good public examination results, and being willing to pull one's weight in after-class activities. At Colander High it is uncommonly difficult to produce good public examination results, and exceedingly tiresome to pull one's weight in after-class activities.

It is difficult for a teacher to impose classroom order at Colander High because his pupils, as we have seen, generally come from homes in which learning is not valued for its own sake, so they have little incentive to exert themselves in academic endeavours, and most of them leave school as soon as the law permits.

There is no family tradition of lengthy education in Colander. Colander High parents are evasive on the subject of their own schooling and it was thought impolitic to press the point. 'Things were very different in my day – I never had much of a chance,' they said. Many explained their poverty in terms of their relative lack of schooling and expounded upon their own experiences as a warning to their children, but none insisted that the children remained at school beyond Standard 8. The lack of family schooling tradition and of parental ambitions for the prolonged training of their children is probably a factor of some importance in determining the early age at which the children leave school. Observers have noted the importance of this factor in other countries.[5]

Most children, in response to a questionnaire conducted in the school, indicated that they desired to leave school 'as soon as possible' – at 16 or 17, which usually means after having passed Standard 8. Just under 60 per cent said they would take up employment immediately on leaving school and without further training. Just under 30 per cent indicated that they would be taking evening classes at technical college, studying a trade or shorthand/typing. Eight per cent expected to study full-time at a technical college. None expected to go to university. A handful were 'not sure', or thought they would stay at home.

Such pupils think school a waste of time and, being thus frustrated, are in no mood to co-operate with their teachers. They continually contrive ways to interrupt the work of the class, and seek assiduously for every chink in their teachers' armour. Once they have found it, they torment them mercilessly: at any one time there is likely to be near-uproar in at least one classroom in the school. In such circumstances a disproportionate number of teachers acquire a reputation for being unable to cope with 'discipline'; henceforth they are not 'good' teachers, and have little hope of promotion to a 'good' school.

A teacher who is 'good' at his job produces 'results', that is, his pupils do well in public examinations. Colander High teachers do not obtain such results in public examinations. The difficulty of maintaining order, the lack of incentive in pupils, and pupils' low IQ may partly account for this failure.

A 'good' teacher – as defined by teachers – takes a keen interest in his school's games, clubs, and cultural societies. His keenness to participate in such activities is a measure of the rewards he experiences. He can, if keen, expect commendation from his Principal and from the Inspectors, but more important than such juicy carrots are the minor but cumulative daily gratifications he is likely to experience: the insight he gains into the characters of his pupils, the gratitude of children, the pride of seeing an otherwise undistinguished scholar making his mark in the Gilbert and Sullivan production. These things are largely denied the Colander High teacher. Once the last bell of the day has rung, his pupils' only thought is to quit the school premises and they resent being coerced into remaining for additional organized activities. The English Public School keenness for games, for best-speaker debates, and for other such middle-class delights is foreign to them; and such enthusiasm as they have is expended on soccer and baseball rather than on the games they are encouraged to play – rugby football and cricket. With such material to work with, no teacher can hope to make a name for himself as a coach, for games successes are few. Besides, to visit the playing fields of a more popular school in the company of one's team can be a humiliating experience: colleagues might maintain a discreet silence, but their pupils are unlikely to allow the swarthy skins and down-at-heel attire of the Colander High team to escape comment. Not unnaturally, most Colander High teachers come to regard the supervision of games and societies as an unpleasant chore to be avoided where possible. So ambitious teachers do not by preference seek appointment at Colander High; still less do they desire to remain there. And since teachers are in short supply, and 'good' teachers even more so, it is generally left to those of modest ambition and small potential to teach at the school.

Such is the 'bad name' of the school, and such is the risk which a good teacher runs in being associated with it, that teachers have been warned unofficially by officials of the Department of Education and by lecturers of teacher-training institutions not to seek appointment there. The Vice-Principal of the school himself advises recruits against remaining: 'Bishops, Rustenburg, Rondebosch: these are the schools that matter. Once you've been at Colander High for a while you'll never move up; so if you have any ambition, take the opportunity when it comes.' The Principal is left to lament:

> Replies to advertisements for teachers are conspicuous by their absence. Often we consider ourselves fortunate if we receive a single reply for a vacancy. . . . New teachers coming to our school soon realize the enormity of their task and have no difficulty in obtaining posts in schools where the work is far less exacting – the material being much superior. Also, they soon learn that positions in the more privileged areas are infinitely better stepping-stones to promotion. They have no real reason for remaining with us and soon leave.

The extreme unpopularity of the school among teachers results in a high turnover of tiros, some indication of which is provided in school records. The ratio of teachers having 'temporary' appointments to those having 'permanent' appointments for the years 1956–1960 vary between 2 : 10 and 4 : 9.

Of the 13 teachers of 'permanent' status who resigned from their posts during the period under review, 5 had remained at the school for no more than a year and 7 others for less than five years. Such figures provide only an incomplete idea of the rate of turnover, for they give no account of the turnover of what are probably the most mobile categories of teachers: itinerants, part-timers, and temporary replacements for those on sick leave. School records concerning these categories are sketchy, but they do imply an extremely high rate of mobility. For example, no less than five temporary mathematics teachers were hired in 1958.

Not all the teachers on the staff are so mobile. Six long-term teachers had between them completed 91 years of service at the school by the end of 1960. Some of them came to the school when it had not yet acquired the bad name it now has, and at a time, moreover, when the number of teachers applying for posts exceeded the number of posts available. To them it was no dishonour to be associated with Colander High. They have remained for various reasons: some have stayed because they are of working-class background, feel at ease among working-class children, and unhappy at more popular schools; some because their lengthy stay has been rewarded with a seniority which they are unlikely to win elsewhere; others because they know of no better school which will have them, either because their social background (Catholic or working-class) is unacceptable, or because their professional qualifications are minimal.[6] All have the handicap in the race for promotion to more popular schools of having been associated with Colander High. The longer they stay at the school, the more difficult it is for them to leave it.

The categories 'long-term teacher' and 'tiro' provide the basis for the informal organization of the staff. Both groups of teachers find themselves in an unrewarding situation in which, like members of coercive institutions,[7] they experience frustration and alienation, and from which they desire to escape. But their reactions to the situation differ because, while tiros are able to quit the school, the long-term teachers are not. A description of these differing reactions follows.

Recruits are absorbed in small numbers, and their relative inexperience renders them vulnerable to pressures exerted by long-term teachers; so they lack the cohesion of their elders, and are leaderless. Nevertheless, there is a diffuse camaraderie among tiros, fellows in misfortune. This camaraderie is partly a result of their rejection by the long-term teachers, partly of shared task-related problems, and partly of similarity of age. Also binding tiros together and setting them apart from their elders are certain sentiments and attitudes which they hold in common. Some of these attitudes, especially relatively liberal attitudes concerning classroom control, are related to tiros' relatively recent professional training. The innovations to which such attitudes give rise are rejected by the long-term teachers as implicit criticisms of the existing hierarchy, which in part is seen as reflecting relative competence in older methods of teaching. Other attitudes held in common by tiros are related to the fact that they have little or no stake in the school. Recruits generally intend to leave Colander High as soon as they conveniently can, for their identification with a working-class and White school is an embarrassment to them. They regard the school with distaste, and have little incentive to develop loyalty towards it.

Few words mean so much to teachers as does 'loyalty'. 'Loyalty' means supporting one's colleagues in the face of pupils, parents, the School Committee, members of other schools, bureaucrats – and even, on occasion, the Principal. It means not courting popularity with pupils at the expense of other teachers; not discussing, in the presence of pupils or parents, the personal affairs of other teachers, or casting doubt upon their ability to enforce 'discipline'; not revealing enmities and schisms in the staff-room to outsiders; not obtrusively hunting promotion by currying favour with the Principal if this action shows up competitors in a poor light; not running down the school by word of mouth, or lowering its prestige by meriting obloquy through scandalous conduct of one's personal affairs.

Solidarity in the face of pupils is perceived as a cardinal virtue. No teacher is more despised or feared than one who interrupts another's class to issue a trivial command, unless it is one who encourages pupils to confide in him which teachers they dislike or which they can goad with impunity. 'Loyal' teachers support each other in enforcing 'discipline'; they even co-ordinate marks they award for work completed by pupils, lest disparate marks lead pupils to smell division among the staff. Solidarity in the face of parents is thought equally desirable. During public ceremonies teachers sit together, segregated from parents as much as from pupils, and they exchange scornful remarks about parents, just as they do about pupils. Parental complaints, whether made verbally or through the daily press, are derisively brushed aside. Solidarity is maintained in the face of all outsiders – School Committees, School Boards, and School Inspectors: Inspectors are informed by the Principal, tongue in cheek, that he 'enjoys the full co-operation of the staff, who show a genuine interest in their pupils' welfare and in the work of the school'. Even the teachers of other schools are not proof against the staff's solidarity: such may be mocked, but one's own colleagues are beyond reproach. Teachers feel that only by concerted action and mutual support can they meet the threats to their powers and authority.

Tiros are not 'loyal' to the school. The status anxiety which many experience as upwardly mobile persons is increased manyfold by identification with a working-class and pass-White school; and they know that their connection with Colander High will be no advantage to them when they come to apply for positions at more popular schools. They hope their stay will be short-lived. Meanwhile, they attempt to minimize their association with Colander High. They shun forging links with parents or children, they do not visit pupils' homes, they cold-shoulder the PTA and Old Pupils' Association. At best they let it be known that they see themselves as missionaries of the middle classes among a fallen people: they wish their scholars to talk, dress, and comport themselves in a manner befitting the middle classes; they want to 'spread a little beauty' into the lives of those whose misfortune it is to come from a 'terrible background'. At worst, they malign the community and blacken the school. Some even protest that their colleagues are not fit to associate with – that they wear bloomers, or take snuff, or are unwashed. Said one, '[the physical training teacher] has a job getting some of the boys to shower. I don't know how he stands it. There are some teachers like that.' All make it their business to inform their friends and colleagues that their stay is temporary and, however fleeting, distasteful to them.

Tiros have no stake in the school. They adapt their behaviour accordingly and become apathetic. They take little interest in their pupils, make no attempt to acquaint themselves with their hopes and ambitions. They affect indifference to school games and societies, even to purely academic work. 'It is best not to interest yourself in the children,' declared one, 'because if you do you would have to work yourself to death.' Such apathy does not endear them to their pupils, who react by withdrawing co-operation and by continually sniping at teachers' authority. Tiros in turn react by imposing progressively more authoritarian forms of control and this merely intensifies the hostility of the children.

Long-term teachers, unlike tiros, are not transient. They have none of them remained at the school out of choice, and their greatest desire is to be promoted *out* of the school; but since they are there they have to make the best of it. Anything they do or say which brings the school or its community into disrepute affects them more intimately than it affects temporary teachers: they have a stake in the system. It is to their advantage to create as favourable an image as possible of the school so that their own prestige may be enhanced and the school attract both more and 'better' pupils. So they are 'loyal' to the school. It is the long-term teachers who, in times gone by, arranged for school gatherings to be addressed by Superintendents-General of Education, Ministers of Education, and Mayors; who organized Eisteddfods, elocution classes, and Scout Jamborees; who edited a school magazine which contained belles lettres and articles on Carlyle and Nelson. It is they who today complain most bitterly when boys come to school with long hair and unpolished shoes, or when girls dye their hair and wear high heels. It is they, in sum, who are most concerned with 'raising the tone' of the school.

Long-term teachers are afraid that some of the working-class image of Colander might rub off on them, but they cannot dissociate themselves altogether from the suburb. Their protestations that they do not belong to it have a hollow ring, and carry much less conviction than those made by teachers whose sojourn at the school is brief, so they do not make the kind of disparaging remarks about parents and children so characteristic of tiros: they are, in relation to outsiders, 'loyal' to Colander.

These long-term teachers, not surprisingly, have a virtual monopoly of formal powers among the staff. Among their number is the Principal, the Vice-Principal, and the Special-Grade Assistant. They occupy all strategic positions within the school, such as librarian, editor of the school magazine, and masters in charge of cricket, rugby football, tennis, cadets, and detention classes. They take charge of morning assembly, occupy the most strategic seats in the staff-room, and represent the school in negotiations with outside bodies. Likewise they have a monopoly of privileges. They lead the procession into morning assembly, sit where they like in the staff-room, have their tea poured out for them by tiros, and teach the higher standards and more congenial classes. Their powers and privileges derive largely from their length of service at the school. The rapid turnover of recruits makes it possible – and indeed necessary – for long-term teachers to capture positions of power and privilege and to entrench themselves in them.

These powers and privileges are maintained partly by mechanisms designed to check any challenge to the *status quo*. Primary among these mechanisms is the process of socialization to which the long-term teachers subject recruits. This takes at first the form of rebuffing a recruit's friendly overtures until he realizes that he is a nonentity in the staff-room and that any ideas he has of his own importance must be forgotten. The process is akin to the suppressing of previous statuses of recruits to a military academy, as described in a well-known paper by Dornbusch.[8] For example, the superior academic qualification held by a tiro came to be reduced to those of other staff members holding no more than a matriculation certificate on the grounds that his academic status was anomalous with his status as the most junior of junior teachers: the anomaly had to be resolved by devaluing his university connection. The task was accomplished by the Vice-Principal, who intoned:

> I have two degrees, and I could easily have got a Ph.D. My professor told me not to hand in my work for an M.A.: Save it for a Ph.D., he said. But I wasn't interested. It means nothing. Some people just go on collecting degrees for the sake of their ego.

The recruit's requests for information and for help in adjusting himself to an unfamiliar task are tacitly ignored so that he soon becomes aware of the power of the long-term teachers and of his need to ingratiate himself with them. Should he react by making the required submissive gestures, such as sitting in the least popular chairs at elevenses, pouring tea, and deferring to the opinions of his seniors, fatherly advice will be lavished on him, and he will be drawn ostentatiously into conversation. He will learn, among other things, to adopt the 'right' attitude to work (not appearing over-keen); the 'right' way of maintaining classroom order ('keeping them under your thumb'); and will acquire a lighthearted manner of dismissing educational psychology, and a cynicism concerning parents, pupils, and bureaucrats who 'don't know the difference between bed and B.Ed.'.

This process will take half a year, during which time the recruit remains, as it were, safely quarantined. Once he returns for a second term, however, and the long-term teachers realize that he intends to stay for at least a year and is not merely another fly-by-night, the staff-room atmosphere undergoes a subtle change. He is still treated with circumspection, but he comes to be regarded as one of Us rather than of Them. Then, at long last, he is let into the dreadful secret that the Principal is thought to be incompetent; he is induced to conspire against him in some minor but meaningful act of rebellion (the retailing of malicious gossip concerning him suffices); this done, he has been, like his colleagues, rendered unclean, for he has broken the most awful injunction of the staff-room – he has been 'disloyal'. In this way he becomes united with his colleagues in their tacit opposition to the Principal and in the pedagogic simulacrum of a state of ritual impurity.

The process is not infallible, for some tiros are too proud or too fractious to submit to the oligarchy. These become the objects of witch-hunts. Teachers are subjected to continual conflicts which appear to them intractable, if only because, as Wayne Gordon has it,

> The success ideology of the school states that 'successful teachers do not have problems', therefore the most disturbing problems of the teacher tend to be regarded as unique to his situation and therefore as private. His greatest anxieties are not expressed. The teacher perspective with its failure to incorporate the reality of the social structure in which he works prevents him from seeing problems as a consequence of this generic structure.[9]

Teachers attempt to solve their difficulties by sacrificing a scapegoat: the Principal, being the school incarnate, is an obvious target for pent-up aggression, yet he is not a convenient one, for he can retaliate: a defenceless victim is therefore sought among recruits. Such a victim is almost invariably an enthusiastic teacher whose ambitious projects would increase the work of the long-term teachers beyond what they are prepared to contemplate, or whose academic attainment, understanding of educational psychology, or teaching skill, illuminates their deficiencies. The excuse for settling upon such a one as a victim is usually found in his difficulty in maintaining good order in the classroom; for new teachers, being inexperienced, often encounter such difficulties. As Parsons has noted, 'Scapegoating . . . rarely appears without *some* 'reasonable' basis of antagonism in that there is a real conflict of ideals or interests'.[10] 'Disciplinary' problems, endemic to the school, are blamed upon the tiro and he is driven, like the Gadarene swine, out of the school. The Principal describes one who became a scapegoat:

> . . . an unqualified inexperienced young man who tried to teach mathematics and who, himself, has only secured a Senior Certificate. He had a great opinion of himself, was able to criticize everything and everybody, even the Inspector and the Principal, and remarked on the 'easiness' of the papers in mathematics. He claimed to have answered the first paper in 15 minutes! The results of our candidates with this subject were Bad.
>
> Thus the 'true' teachers of the senior classes had an additional burden and responsibility – namely, of trying to maintain the dignity of the teacher's position and to hold the respect of the pupils.

The expulsion of a scapegoat is a simple process. All that is required to make a recruit feel so unwelcome as to resign voluntarily is that other teachers should fall silent as he enters the staff-room, should ignore his pleas for aid, should flagrantly change the subject while he is in mid-sentence, and should discuss his shortcomings in a tone loud enough for him to overhear. By means of the witch-hunt the group is cleansed of a deviate, solidarity is enhanced, frustrated feelings are given vent, and the tiros are cowed into submission. No tiro dare step out of line for fear of being smelt out; and no colleague dare protect him for fear of contamination by association. This is the way the tiros are kept divided, and one of the ways in which the long-term teachers maintain their rule.

Mrs Smith provides an example of a scapegoat. After having reared three children, she returned to teaching in order to earn pin-money. As an experienced teacher and an older woman she appeared to consider herself the peer of the long-term teachers and it was with them rather than with tiros that she initially attempted to mix. Her reception was polite but cool, but this did not inhibit her effervescent conversation. After a week's stay at the school her demeanour, in marked contrast to that of a young tiro recruited contemporaneously with her, was no less animated. At about this time long-term teachers began trying to freeze her out of conversation but she did not appear to notice and persisted in pressing her company on them. The rebuffs to which she was increasingly subjected grew brazen. Not only did whispered exchanges come to an abrupt halt when she entered the staff-room but her friendly overtures were ignored point blank. When she twice requested the Vice-Principal for the use of a wall-map for her class and her requests were studiously ignored, her nerve began to break. She sought solace in the company of tiros at the other end of the room. The writer, for one, regarded her warily, for I was fearful of incurring the wrath of my seniors. Her recourse to the society of tiros did not escape the attention of her persecutors and they moved quickly to deprive her of this source of comfort. Whenever she opened conversation with a tiro, long-term teachers ostentatiously winked at each other and at the tiro and began complaining to tiros, in her absence, of the increased difficulty they were experiencing in maintaining order among the classes she taught. That she might be blamed for such disorder never, apparently, occurred to her, for she publicly lamented her inability to cope with 'dreadful' working-class pupils. She solicited my advice. I suggested, as tactfully as I could, that, in accordance with staff ideology, she should 'stand no nonsense'. When she left the room I was astonished to find myself being congratulated by the Special-Grade Assistant for 'giving her a good dressing-down'. In the end – not more than half way through term – the atmosphere in the staff-room became so tense that Mrs Smith took to having her tea in solitude, in an empty classroom. The end of term saw her departure from the school and that, teachers agreed, was 'the best thing she could have done'.

The literature on witchcraft and scapegoating provides abundant parallels to the case of Mrs Smith.[11] Many writers have observed that in groups in which realistic conflict is inhibited[12] or in which frustrations are imposed by sources difficult to define or locate[13] there exists a tendency to displace hostility on to some vulnerable individual of low status. Moreover there is evidence to indicate that 'The larger the proportion of new members joining an established group within a given period of time (short of actually taking it over), the greater will be the resistance of the group to their assimilation.[14] The case of Mrs Smith is, however, in one respect, unusual: she is but one of four tiros driven out of the school within a period of three years. The long-term teachers, being captive to the school, face perennial frustrations and so have need of a perennial number of semi-stranger scapegoats.

It is instructive to note that the conduct of recruits in process of being absorbed into the group is very different from that of teachers who are itinerant or who are temporarily replacing those on sick-leave. Such rolling stones are immune to the depredations of the long-term teachers and so are free to sit where they will, to talk when they will, and to hold forth without hindrance on any subject that takes their fancy.

NOTES

1 W. W. Waller, *The Sociology of Teaching*, New York, John Wiley, 1932.

2 According to the *Report of the Superintendent-General of Education, 1960*, the actual shortage of secondary teachers in the Cape Province for 1960 was 626 out of 3,183. Similar shortages are mentioned in almost every edition of the *Report* published since the war.

3 The relationship between measured intelligence and innate capacity is a controversial issue. Many writers have attempted to demonstrate that IQ tests have biases built into them favourable to upper- and middle-class students. See, for example, K. Eells, *et al.*, *Intelligence and Cultural Differences*, Chicago, University of Chicago Press, 1951.

4 Teachers seeking employment answer advertisements in the *Education Gazette*. Their applications are considered by the relevant School Committee,

in consultation with the Principal Teacher. If an application is approved it has to be ratified by the School Board.

5 See, for example, J. E. Floud, A. H. Halsey, and F. M. Martin, *Social Class and Educational Opportunity*, London, Heinemann, 1956.

6 All the permanent teachers on the staff are certified teachers. Two have degrees at the Master level and five at the Bachelor level. Two have no higher academic qualification than a senior school-leaving certificate.

7 For a discussion of the social psychology of coercive institutions see A. Etzioni, *A Comparative Analysis of Complex Organizations*, Glencoe, The Free Press, 1961.

8 S. M. Dornbusch, 'The Military Academy as an Assimilating Institution', *Social Forces*, Vol. 33, pp. 316–21.

9 C. W. Gordon, 'The Role of the Teacher in the Social Structure of the High School', *Journal of Educational Sociology*, Vol. 29, Sept. 1955, pp. 21–9.

10 T. Parsons, *Religious Perspectives of College Teaching in Sociology and Social Psychology*, New Haven, The Edward W. Hagen Foundation, 1951, p. 40.

11 See, for example, P. Mayer, *Witchcraft*, Inaugural Lecture to the Rhodes University, Grahamstown, South Africa, 1954. A good critical examination of the literature on scapegoating is in Chapter 6 of J. W. Vander Zanden, *American Minority Relations* (Second edition), New York, Ronald Press, 1966.

12 See L. Coser, *The Functions of Social Conflict*, London, Routledge and Kegan Paul, 1956, *passim*.

13 See R. M. Williams, Jr., *The Reduction of Intergroup Tensions*, New York, Social Science Research Council, 1943, Ch. 3.

14 B. Berelson and G. Steiner, *Human Behavior: An Inventory of Scientific Findings*, New York, Harcourt, Brace and World, 1964, p. 330.

Chapter Eight

PRINCIPAL AND VICE-PRINCIPAL

The formal organization of the teachers of Colander High consists of a simple chain of command, in accordance with that laid down in the Education Ordinance, of Principal Teacher, Vice-Principal, Special-Grade Assistant, Assistant Teachers, and Teachers-in-Training. At the apex of the organizational hierarchy is the Principal Teacher; and his role, as baldly outlined in the Ordinance, is that he shall 'supervise and direct the work of the school', and that he shall act as liaison between the teaching staff, on the one hand, and the community and bureaucracy, on the other. He has as his lieutenant a Vice-Principal, 'who shall discharge such special duties, apart from his normal duties as a member of the staff, as may be assigned to him from time to time by the principal teacher'.

The roles outlined in the Ordinance are no more than the skeletons around which has accumulated a good deal of flesh. For the moment it will suffice merely to note the salient features of this flesh. A Principal Teacher who is thought by teachers to fulfil his role adequately is much more than a supervisor and director: he is a skilled and experienced pedagogue, an efficient administrator, a trenchant disciplinarian, a consummate diplomat, a perceptive judge of human nature; above all, he is a forceful leader. A Vice-Principal who wins the respect of his staff shares many of the qualities of a Principal, and is equipped to assume the office of supervisor and director whenever necessary. He carries much of the burden of routine administration and is a Principal's chief lieutenant.

The incumbents of the roles of Principal and Vice-Principal at Colander High do not play their roles according to the script. The Principal is by no means a forceful leader. The Vice-Principal has a domineering character, and his loyalty to the Principal is fickle. The thesis which will be advanced in the following pages is that this situation is very largely a function of the school's relation to its community.

The Principal is a kindly bird-like man with the air of a zealous but ineffectual missionary. He is quite lacking in grandeur and his accent alone would disqualify him in the race for the principalship of a popular school. He came to Colander over thirty years ago, a Master of Arts, and in possession of a teachers' diploma. Later he succeeded to the principalship and set about his new job with considerable enthusiasm. He wanted the school, he said, to be 'a special school'. Now his enthusiasm has dimmed and he has applied to the School Board for a transfer. 'He's been here too long,' says the caretaker. 'Ten years of this are too much for any man.'

His situation is not a happy one. Most of his time in school hours is spent on clerical work, making out reports to the Department, or filling in forms for the School Board. His relations with these bodies is not gratifying, and the tone of the correspondence he addresses to them is most often sullen, even acrimonious. Of the Department he says 'It's got no heart. It's got no soul. It's got no feeling. That's all there is to it. As long as you've made out the forms they want that is all they're interested in. They pat you on the back, but that achieves nothing.' He has no friends among his staff, and relations with his Vice-Principal are fraught with friction. Parents he seldom sees ('It's a nuisance when the mothers come') except when he has to establish their racial status at an initial traumatic interview or when they come to the office to voice a complaint. ('I have to tell them to get out or I will get out, and I have to do it and that is not the sort of thing a Principal should have to do.') Ask a mother of a Colander High pupil if she has met him and one receives the characteristic indignant reply, 'There has never been any trouble at school!' He addresses children at morning assembly but almost his only opportunity of making pleasurable personal contact with them is during informal classes which he conducts; and this he lives for. If he meets children on the personal level at other times, as likely as not it will be to administer severe reprimands or corporal punishment on behalf of his staff or School Committee. The children's academic records, their general indifference to religious and middle-class values, the 'terrible' homes from which they come – these things fill him with despair. Not surprisingly, he is described by his wife as being 'very often depressed about the school'.

He lives comfortably on his salary a dozen miles from the school, in a somewhat pretentious suburb. There he is a well-known public figure. But he takes no part at all in the local affairs of Colander. He would like to teach nearer his home, and might have realized his ambition when a local School Committee forwarded his candidature

H

for the principalship of their school to the School Board. The Board turned him down in favour of a candidate who had had no experience even as a Vice-Principal. He was downcast. 'You know what the Board said? "We need Mr Jones at Colander High." They can't get anybody else to come here – at least, not to do what I'm doing. I have given them 30 years, and this is how they treat me: I had hoped to end my career in a different atmosphere.'

He is not held in high esteem by his teaching staff. Conversations with teachers in Cape Town indicate that they expect a Principal to be a 'strong' man, an undisputed leader, a man who wins the respect of his Vice-Principal: under such a man teachers hope to be spared being drawn into the conflicts of those who aspire to fill the power vacuum such as is left by a vacillating Principal. Teachers expect a Principal to impose a firm discipline on his charges: under such a man their ever-latent fears of classroom disorder are dispelled. Teachers expect their Principal to back them up in relation to outsiders, to ward off parents who attempt to dictate how teachers shall teach or how they shall treat mummy's darling, and to rebuff officious representatives of the School Committee or School Board who threaten to erode their autonomy: under such a man they feel their professional status secure. Teachers expect their Principal to be a man of stature who 'builds up the good name of the school', a man of influence, adept at persuading bureaucrats to open their coffers: under such a man they attract the envy of their colleagues and bask in the esteem of the community. The Principal of Colander High is not able to live up to such expectations; his relations with parents and bureaucrats all but ensure that. He is constrained to refuse admission to dark-complexioned children, thus attracting the resentment of parents and of the School Committee. ('It has halved my Christian influence.') On the other hand, he is obliged to accept 'difficult' pupils and pass-Whites sent him by the School Board. Resistance earns the Board's censure; the inevitable capitulation earns the mistrust of his staff and of the Department of Education. He is a striking instance of the *middle man*, in whom, as Gluckman notes, 'the frailty of conflicting authority is strong'.[1] He embodies the 'conflict between the ideals of leadership and the weakness of the leader'.[2]

Compounding his tribulations is the character of the scholars which the school attracts. The fact that these children are mostly working-class, and hence of low social status, is in itself sufficient to condemn the school to low social status and precludes his efforts to earn the school a 'good name' and the kind of facilities found at more favoured schools. The working-class parents of the children lack the money and the influence necessary to acquire as much as a playing field for the school, the purchase of which would be subsidized by the Department of Education on the pound-for-pound principle. Thirty years after its inception, Colander High still lacks a single playing field. 'It's just that we haven't got people around here who can say "Come and have a drink with me and talk it over",' he complains. The children are generally indifferent or hostile to academic excellence, and their boredom and frustration, taken together with a working-class culture which permits of the relatively unrestrained expression of aggressive impulses, makes for classroom turmoil and teachers' discontent. And because the school lacks a 'good name' it is generally unable to attract teachers who rank high in the estimation of their colleagues; and this fact further confirms the school in its ill-repute. Since, for the same reason, teachers are tempted to quit the school, he dare not assert his authority vigorously lest he antagonize his staff and so encourages them to succumb to temptation. He confesses: 'I leave my staff alone as much as possible because they have so many problems of their own – coming from below – from the children – that if I were to exert pressure on them from above they would give it up as a bad job and leave.' With this assessment of the situation his caretaker concurs:

> He lets everybody shit on him because you can't get teachers nowadays. He's lucky if he gets one reply to an advertisement in the Gazette. When [the previous Principal] was here things were different: he didn't stand nonsense from anybody. If you didn't like it he showed you the door. But in those days teachers could go for months – or even years – without a job.

But his teachers are not grateful for his indulgence and they bemoan his 'pathetic inability to put his bloody foot down'. Little wonder he complains that 'other Principals think there is something wrong with me for staying here'.

The reluctance of teachers to apply for jobs at his school deprives him of an important means for controlling staff – control through recruitment. He is left with what he perceives as second-rate staff on whom he places the blame for the rowdiness endemic to the school. He says (in confidence) of two that 'they let their classes do what they want'. Of another he says that his detention classes are 'a picnic'; of another that her classes 'are not as they should be', of another that 'he lets the girl classes run away with him'; of another that she 'is having trouble'; of another that 'he has them under his thumb – but they don't like him'.

He is unable to build up a 'good name' for his school, and so merits the disdain of his teachers. Yet, disdained though he may be, he is not the mere butt of his staff. His very office lends him a not inconsiderable measure of authority. And he can make life difficult for a disrespectful teacher; he can assign an unpopular class to him, refuse to administer corporal punishment on his behalf, neglect to protect him from the unwelcome sallies of irate parents. He can fail to recommend him for promotion, he can forward a damaging report to the Inspectors, and – most dreaded of all – can slate him when potential employers inquire. So, while he is not respected by all, he is feared by all; and while his staff may snipe covertly at his authority, they draw back from confronting him with open rebellion.

The relationship between long-term teachers and tiros has been adumbrated, as has the relationship between the Principal and his staff: what remains to be described is the relationship between, on the one hand, the Vice-Principal and Principal, and, on the other, the Vice-Principal and the rank and file of teachers.

The Vice-Principal has a more forceful personality than the Principal. There is something of the patriarch about him, and at the sound of his martial voice staff-room conversation peters out and a respectful silence ensues. He is a Master of Arts, and the author of a school text. With such notable capabilities (relative to those of his colleagues) it is curious that he has remained at Colander High almost as long as the Principal Teacher, and that he has not succeeded in winning a principalship for himself. He has applied for executive posts at other schools – and even for the Chair of Education at a university – but every attempt to gain promotion has been balked: he is a Catholic and has anti-Catholicism to contend with. 'I applied for a post at the university,' he recounts bitterly, 'but a man without my qualifications got the job. I tried again and again, and in the end went to the man concerned and said; "Look, my qualifications were higher than that fellow's, so let me know if I'm wasting my time and I won't bother to apply again." He said, "All right, you are a better man than he is. You are more highly qualified and have more teaching experience, so it can't be because of that. You know what is left." ' As for his status at Colander High: 'He's been sitting upstairs for years waiting for the principalship to fall into his lap,' says the caretaker; 'but he won't get it. They'll let him act when the chief is away: but he's a Catholic.'

He is embittered with the teaching profession: he protests that salaries are scandalously low; that teachers are hedged about with petty restrictions; that they are subject to surveillance by insolent laymen;

and, most pungently, that they lack 'professional status'. ('Doctors and lawyers don't have to run bazaars.') 'Still teaching?' he demands of old colleagues: 'Surely not for the love of it!' And to tiros he gives this unsolicited advice: 'Never take a fixed job like teaching – look where I am.'

His duties as Vice-Principal are cursorily defined in the Ordinance as 'such duties as may be delegated to him by the Principal Teacher, with the approval of the Committee'. Ask members of staff what these duties are and they will reply that he administers the school library and stockroom, trains the cricket team, makes up the weekly attendance register, and assumes the post of Acting Principal when necessary. All these tasks, except those bound up with the acting principalship, could as well be done by an Assistant Teacher. His is what the journal of the local teachers' association describes as a 'twilight status'. He is the odd man out, the minister without portfolio.

What, apart from his title and superior remuneration, differentiates him from other teachers? It is the expectation that he shall supervise and direct. To conform adequately to this expectation he must win the respect of his subordinates and the support of his Principal. Without the support of his Principal his status is insecure, even untenable. There are many schools in which the Vice-Principal is a nonentity, firmly under the thumb of a mere Assistant Teacher who has usurped the patronage of the Principal. But despite such hazards and susceptibilities the Vice-Principal of Colander High is able to maintain his position quite comfortably.

He is able to do so because, paradoxically, his role is loosely defined. As the activities he is expected to perform are not clearly specified in the Ordinance, neither the Principal nor other staff members can very well object that he is growing too big for his shoes.

He is able to do so, in the second place, because the Principal makes it plain as a pike-staff that he is his chief lieutenant. The Principal does this by relaying many messages and orders to the staff through him; by requesting teachers to consult him even after he has satisfied himself that everything is in order; by praising him conspicuously at staff meetings and never openly criticizing him; and by delegating to him tasks (such as the making up of attendance registers) in which he assumes a position of superordination over other teachers.

The Vice-Principal is not passive in the process of shoring up his status. If delegated to convey an instruction to the staff he will walk round to every classroom to inform each teacher individually, often interrupting lessons unnecessarily to do so: he will even go to the length of interrupting a written message being carried round the class-rooms by a pupil, leave his own classroom, and take the message round himself. He is a stickler for the handing in of attendance registers on time and complains loudly if a teacher has been lax in this regard. Not even the Special-Grade Assistant is exempt from his strictures: 'I haven't handed in my register yet and he hasn't said a word to me all day,' he complained.

He implies disapproval of those teachers who, without first consulting him, approach the Principal. Should he observe a teacher guilty of such an irreverent transgression he is likely to accost him while he is consulting the Principal and to monopolize the Principal's attention. Mostly he succeeds in forestalling such transgressions by rarely missing his three o'clock tea in the Principal's office: three o'clock is a time when many teachers find it convenient to consult the Principal. Should he suspect a teacher of successfully evading his blockade he is quick to retaliate with caustic remarks. ('We don't seem to see Mr Grob very often at tea nowadays – he seems to have rather a lot of work to do.') As a result, teachers take care to avoid crossing him. Said one, 'The Vice-Principal probably thinks I'm siding with the Principal against him. I'm making a point of showing him this is not so by doing duties he appoints me, like library duty. By rights he should be doing it.'

At staff meetings he is verbose and voluble, and should a discussion on some matter make little headway he is likely to ask the Principal to postpone a decision 'Until you and I have looked into the matter more thoroughly.' Only he and the Principal have prior access to a staff-meeting agenda: this ensures that teachers have no opportunity of discussing anything beforehand.

He takes full advantage of his status as the Principal's right-hand man to safeguard his position among the staff. He interacts with the Principal more than does any other teacher; and more with him than with any other teacher: he sits next to the Principal at staff meetings, and is ever in and out of the Principal's office. He represents the Principal to the staff, and the staff to the Principal. His favourites he treats to titbits of inside information; his foes are denied them. His favourites find in him a sure advocate of their pleas; his foes' cases are presented tardily and without enthusiasm.

He also represents the school to outsiders. He is personally acquainted with more parents than any other teacher; and he is the only member of staff, other than the Principal, who is invariably present at School Committee meetings. More grandly, he negotiates on behalf of the school with outside bodies, such as other schools, in the absence of the Principal.

His esteem among teachers does not rest solely upon his status as the Principal's lieutenant: he is master of the staff-room in his own right. The reasons for this are several. In the first place he has the advantage over most of the staff in that he comes to the school with a status which rates fairly high in terms of social class. Let others have sandwiches, wrapped in grease-proof paper, for lunch: he has salads, brought to school in a white napkin. He talks of his house, his car, his garden, and his antiques; he draws attention to his advanced university education; his clothes are palpably expensive; he drops names. It seems only fitting that he should have an office to himself, that he should recline in the largest and most comfortable seat in the staff-room, and that he should be in charge of cricket, the school's 'classiest' game.

In the second place, his indefatigable energy and his assiduous intercourse with other teachers have won him a commanding position in the staff-room. He engages in more task-related activities than any other member of staff; he supervises the library and the stock-room, he coaches the cricket team (and occasionally the hockey and rugby football teams) and assists the Principal when required. Teachers almost of necessity interact with him more than with any other member of staff, for he has control of facilities which teachers frequently utilize, and he arranges the roster of duties for teachers in charge of sports' teams and detention classes. In sum, he occupies a strategic position in the staff's communication network. Even in the most informal of situations he is not to be by-passed: in the staff-room he occupies the most commanding position, at the head of the table, whence he is able to survey the entire room and – unlike others – capture the attention of any teacher at will.

He assumes leadership in the formulation and reaffirmation of staff-room mores. His lengthy service has left him with an intimate knowledge of the customs of the staff-room, and he is prompt to chastise the transgressor. ('Come at eight o'clock? You're setting a very bad example: school begins at eight-forty!') It is not simply that his sentiments are always in accord with those of the other teachers: his sentiments are regarded as somehow morally superior – as somehow most proper for a teacher to utter. He provides an instance of the generalization that 'The higher the rank of a person within a group, the more nearly his activities conform to the norms of the group'.[3] For example: teachers complain of the stupidity and the recalcitrance of scholars; he concurs; but he adds some such affirmation as:

True, but we must not be harsh. You may have heard me call some of these boys and girls 'my child': I do that for a reason: they need affection and I give them it. I love these children. That doesn't mean you have to be soft: they won't respect you for that. Some of them come from homes where the mother is out working all day and the father comes home drunk, and they are all left to roam the streets. They don't get affection at home; so we've got to make up for it. It's not a teacher's job – I mean, where's your professional status? – but we've got to do it.

Another pretty example:

In this job you can expect neither professional status nor money: the reward is in the teaching itself. And it is a reward. Like Churchill during the War, all I can offer you is blood, sweat and tears. The people of England accepted. . . .'

Such affirmations, embodying sentiments which teachers feel they ought to share, have the effect of making the rest of the staff reflect guiltily upon their own utterances. For they have much to feel guilty about. It is the custom at Colander High to refer to children only in terms which could not possibly be misconstrued as affectionate. Typically, a teacher enters the staff-room exclaiming some such remark as: 'That boy really is the limit; I gave him a good clout'; or, 'Some of these girls look like street-walkers: they probably are'. Those conversant with the nuances of staff-room usages will interpret the first remark as meaning 'I am a good disciplinarian', and the second as 'These lower-class brats are an affront to my middle-classness'.

The Vice-Principal, as we have already noted, occasionally represents the staff in negotiations with outsiders. He performs an analogous role in the staff-room: he formulates sentiments reflecting the corporate interests of the staff as against those of outsiders. He discourses critically upon the functions and failings of School Inspectors, university lecturers, teachers' associations, School Boards and Committees. The purportedly restrictive and forward role of Inspectors is one of his favourite topics. 'What right have they to scale down our marks if they haven't been teaching the children?' he demands. 'That causes the Principal to lose confidence in his teachers.' Another favourite topic is the alleged difficulty which teachers experience in securing promotion:

That's one thing about teaching: if you want a job, you've got a job. If you do science or carpentry or any of the languages, you can get a job anywhere in the country. Only there are no prospects. It's not right. You've got a job, but where can you go from there? You can't become a Principal. You can only become an Inspector. How many science Inspectors are there in the country? And look at him: he has spent nearly all his life here and all he can do now is become an Inspector of science. It's not fair. What incentive has he got? No matter how well he has taught science or what he has done for the school he will never be transferred. I'm not saying we won't do our best anyway, but it would be nice to think that we might get some recognition for it. They won't move him from here. My friend did a stint at Bishops, then Rondebosch, and a year in the bush to get him into Coloured education; and from there he went right up to headmaster in Rhodesia. Bishops, Rondebosch, Rustenburg – these are the schools that matter. Colander High and the others don't count. Once you've been at Colander High for a while you'll never move up. So, if you want to move on, take the opportunity when it comes. And they won't make a Vice-Principal headmaster of his own school if it's Grade A, B, or C. I know a chap who was Vice-Principal and who acted for a whole year as Principal while the Principal was ill. The Principal resigned in the end, but though the Vice-Principal had run the school well they still wouldn't give him the job. They gave him the post on a temporary basis and advertised it every term, and as soon as another Principal applied, that man got the job. So if you can help to pull the school up, you don't get advancement. If you drag it down you've got a chance. Funny, isn't it? The new Principal comes from a Grade E school: these are the stepping-stones. A few years in Bishops or Rondebosch, and a few more as headmaster of a Grade E, and you're on top.

The Principal's and Vice-Principal's façade of mutual support serves imperfectly to conceal deep-rooted friction between them. This friction has occasionally become public, as it did during the following incidents:

The Vice-Principal was in charge of the school library. The library was due for re-cataloguing, a formidable task. He set about it with little enthusiasm, and after some time had made scant progress. He complained about the amount of work involved, and the Principal immediately relieved him of it. The Principal took the job into his own hands, and, with the help of several children, finished the work in a few days. The Vice-Principal absented himself with a 'severe cold', and the staff hailed the incident as a 'showdown'.

Another incident:

The Vice-Principal was involved in a running feud with the caretaker, and eventually asked the Principal to dismiss his opponent. The Principal refused to do so and, addressing the Vice-Principal, declared, 'If you don't like it, there's the door!' He turned to the caretaker and said (according to the caretaker himself): 'Just keep at arms' length from him. As Vice-Principal he hasn't been one bit of use to me. He hasn't taken one bit of work off my shoulders.' The Vice-Principal absented himself with another 'severe cold'. Teachers observed disingenuously that he appeared quite well when he left.

The Vice-Principal snipes at the authority of the Principal, but without ever doing it openly. However, if he does not overtly criticize the Principal, neither does he praise him. He often complains about something in the school – about 'the general lack of discipline' – the lack of lockers for the staff – the poor standard of pupils coming to the school – or some other matter. Sometimes (too often to be mere chance) such criticism is followed by a series of comments like this: 'It's surprising the difference a headmaster makes to a school. The staff – the Vice-Principal – they can do nothing.' Or, 'They don't seem to make headmasters the way they used to. Look at [Z]: he *was* the school. You couldn't mention the place without thinking of him.' And he eulogizes the school's previous Principal Teacher.

His challenge to the authority of the Principal is even more apparent in his actions than in his words. The Principal irritates most of the staff by failing, in their eyes, to administer the school efficiently. As the Special-Grade Assistant remarks: 'He's a wonderful theorist; but when it comes to putting it into practice he makes a lovely mess of things. Administration . . . hrrmpf!' The Vice-Principal does not hesitate to underline any failure in this respect, thus covertly censuring his senior. His underlining of administrative shortcomings sometimes takes the form of inaction when appropriate action on his part would save the situation. At other times, it takes the form of emphatic, even ostentatious, activity. For example: at the end of the school term, hours were shortened, and some periods interchanged. The result was confusion among staff and scholars, for not all knew what the precise arrangements were, and some had forgotten. The din in the corridors emanating from a bewildered mass of children drew the comments of several teachers, who blithely asked each other – in the presence of the Vice-Principal – why something was not done about it. The Vice-Principal might well have deputed someone – if only a prefect – to restore order; but he chose instead to shrug his shoulders and sigh: 'You had better go and see the Headmaster; I keep out of the way on days like this; I have nothing to do with it.' When, on the other hand, the Vice-Principal does decide to act, he very often does so with great panache. The school becomes a model of efficiency, and it is patent that he is straining every nerve to demonstrate how smoothly the school functions when he is in command. The Principal rarely misses an opportunity of proselytizing Christianity in the school, and this has the effect of antagonizing most of his staff for what they perceive as tiresome religiosity. 'He doesn't have to go on and on and on,' bemoans one teacher. 'I can't even light a cigarette now without thinking I'm committing a mortal sin. I feel as if I'm sinning all the time.' But when the Vice-Principal takes morning assembly, in his capacity as Acting Principal, there is either no mention of religion, or no more than a brief passage read from the Bible without comment.

In his actions and in his words the Vice-Principal implies that he could run the school more efficiently than the Principal. In effect he disclaims responsibility for the school's troubles, places much of the blame on the Principal's shoulders, and persuades the staff that he himself is on their side. In this way he evades such animosity as he might be expected to attract from the staff in view of his middle-man status *vis-à-vis* Principal and staff.

The possibility of friction between a Principal and a Vice-Principal is inherent in the educational system. The Department of Education does not stipulate with any precision what the duties of a Vice-Principal are: this is left largely for his Principal to decide. A Vice-Principal is thought of as being second-in-command, and must strive to maintain a rank superior to that of Assistant Teachers: without the support of his Principal this is probably not possible. A Vice-Principal is therefore dependent on the patronage of his Principal. But, in a sense, he is also the Principal's rival. To further his ambitions he must catch the eye of the circuit Inspector and of the School Committee, and this he can do only by so shining at his work that the Principal may fear being over-shadowed. There is a conflict between his career commitment (which may require angling for promotion out of the school) and his organiza-tional commitment (which requires his not outshining the Principal).

Yet there need not be enmity between Principal and Vice-Principal. There are schools in which the Vice-Principal is a staunch ally and firm friend of the Principal, and there are others in which the Vice-Principal is an innocuous nonentity and the Principal is undisputed master. But the possibility of enmity becomes a probability when a school's relations with its community are such as to diminish the authority of a Principal considerably without affecting that of his Vice-Principal to the same degree, thus producing a situation in which formally granted power becomes divorced from informal authority. The Principal of Colander High loses esteem among his teacher-followers because he fails in enabling them to achieve their desire to acquire a 'good name' for the school and because he fails in his role-specific task of shielding them from incursions upon their field of competence by persons who are not colleagues, while the authority of his Vice-Principal remains unimpaired.

To elaborate, the picture which teachers have of a Principal who is successful in promoting their objectives is one of a man who builds up a favourable image of the school so that it is well patronized by the community and is favoured by the bureaucracy. Under such a Principal bureaucrats listen sympathetically to requests for the creation of additional teaching posts at the school, and are ready to dip into the coffers to subsidize a new school hall, a swimming pool, or playing field. Under such a Principal parents take an active interest in the school, form a co-operative Parent–Teacher Association, run an industrious School Committee, and turn prizegiving day into a gala occasion: but they do not attempt to run the school. They help the children with homework, but they do not jib at the teachers' methods of instruction. They raise funds for the purchase of playing fields, but they do not attempt to dictate what games shall be played on them. They clap enthusiastically at prizegiving ceremonies, hardly questioning the teachers' evaluation of their children. The picture which the teachers of Colander High have of their Principal is one of a man continually at loggerheads with parents and bureaucrats. He has earned the enmity of bureaucrats, parents, and local church leaders over pass-Whites. The School Committee are apathetic, often failing to reach a quorum. Prizegiving ceremonies are ill-attended.[4] Attempts to keep alive the Literary Society, the Knitting Circle, the Red Cross Detachment, the Parent–Teacher Association, and the Past Pupils' Union have all proved abortive. 'We had to do everything for them,' complains the Principal. 'There were only a few who were interested enough to run things themselves. Besides, can you imagine me lecturing to these people on the psychology of adolescence? We showed them film cartoons and conjuring tricks.' School fêtes, organized to raise money for sports equipment and the like, were discontinued because teachers tired of doing all the work themselves, and because the thought of fowls cackling in the school hall proved too much for them. Besides, complain the teachers, parents did not enter into the spirit of the thing: they came early to snap up garden produce at less than market price but ignored the hoopla and tombola. Bureaucrats give short shrift to the Principal's demands for additional staff or for increased remuneration for his teachers. They have given him scant support in his search for playing fields. They send him difficult 'doubtful cases', and regard him with suspicion and hostility when he bows to their demands and accepts them. From the point of view of the teachers, things could hardly be worse.

All this strengthens the hand of the Vice-Principal. He is not held responsible for the outrageous fortune which besets the school. He joins with the staff in grumbling about pass-Whites, about the shortage of teachers, the poor quality of recruits, the administrative muddle, the absence of playing fields. No matter how loudly the Principal protests that he is powerless to improve matters, the suspicion sticks that he is in some way responsible for this sorry state of affairs. And parents as well as teachers grant the Vice-Principal an indulgence which they deny the Principal. On one occasion, after the Vice-Principal had harangued a meeting of parents on some matter, the Principal confided, 'That speech had to come from him. It couldn't have come from me. It was too much of an ultimatum. A Vice-Principal can say things which I can't.'

The upshot is that, while the Principal is head of the formal organization, all but one of the teachers on the staff indicate, by the carping criticism they direct at their Principal but not at their Vice-Principal, that among them the Vice-Principal enjoys by far the greater respect. Of this the Vice-Principal is confident, as the following incident indicates:

> After teachers had all mustered in the staff-room for a staff meeting the Principal entered the room and stood by the door, looking rather helpless. The buzz of conversation did not diminish one whit. Nobody stood up. Nobody offered him a chair. It was as if he were not there. Looking sheepish he began counting the number of teachers present, ending with the comment, 'We seem to be one chair short.' The Vice-Principal started up as if he had only then become aware of the Principal's presence and, not without a hint of ostentation, proffered his chair, which the Principal accepted somewhat awkwardly. He then stood behind the Principal, just as he does during morning assembly – and winked.

The Vice-Principal thus constitutes a challenge to the Principal and the relationship between them is one of considerable strain. They provide an instance of the generalization:

> When authority and responsibility within an organization do not at least roughly correspond to the (perceived) contributions of the members, there is likely to be more than the normal amount of tension within the organization. . . . For example, if lower ranks unduly originate or suggest changes for their superiors, that makes for some strain.[5]

The probability that friction will develop between a Principal and Vice-Principal under the conditions adumbrated becomes a near certainty when a Principal lacks a forceful personality and has as his Vice-Principal a man of incisive character and thwarted ambition. It is no mere quirk of fate that such a situation obtains at Colander

High. The kind of man of sufficient social skill to dominate an unruly staff would be unlikely to remain for long at Colander High, for his services would be in such demand that he would probably have no difficulty in finding a post both more congenial to him and more likely to further his ambitions. And it is not merely fortuitous either that Colander High has a Vice-Principal of such redoubtable character. Were not anti-Catholicism so virulent he would doubtless have long ago won for himself the principalship of a more popular school, but, as it happens, his ambitions are balked and he has little alternative to remaining at the school. And the very fact that he has remained at the school for so long compounds his difficulties in procuring a more congenial post.

How is friction between Principal and Vice-Principal contained? A teacher can be dismissed only after a serious offence (one of those specified in the Ordinance, such as moral turpitude or subversive activity) has been proved to the satisfaction of the School Committee, the School Board, and the Department of Education: under such conditions a dismissal is difficult to effect and easy to evade; so neither the Principal nor the Vice-Principal can oust the other without enormous difficulty. The caretaker has it: 'The chief would jump at the chance of getting rid of [the Vice-Principal] but [the Vice-Principal] always keeps within the letter of the law, and he can do nothing about it.' So the two have to choose between living with each other in open enmity or maintaining such friendly relations as they are able. To choose the course of open enmity would be to court disaster. Neither Principal nor Vice-Principal could hope to emerge unscathed from a process of retaliation and counter-retaliation, since each would undermine the authority of the other. They would suffer loss of esteem in the eyes of their staff: the Principal because he is unable to win the respect of his Vice-Principal, the Vice-Principal because he is 'disloyal' to his Principal. And disaster would not strike solely at the principal belligerents. The staff would feel forced to take sides in a public quarrel between their seniors, and this would have the effect of crystallizing latent factions among the staff. Morale would drop alarmingly, and teachers would leave to escape constant friction. So the friction between Colander High's Principal and Vice-Principal is contained, in the first instance, by the appreciation by all concerned of the disastrous consequences likely to ensue if battle is openly joined.

Friction is contained by two other means: by limiting spheres of potential conflict, and by concealing the extent to which conflict in fact occurs.[6] The Vice-Principal takes no part in cultivating the 'spiritual welfare' of the pupils or in the training of the rugby team – these are the Principal's preserves. In turn, the Principal generally permits the Vice-Principal to manage the library and the cricket team without hindrance. In this way much friction is averted. Such friction as is not successfully averted is mostly kept from the ears of the teachers, and most would be astonished to learn how bitter is the feud between their superordinates. Thus, friction between Principal and Vice-Principal is largely prevented from spreading to the rank and file and so from assuming unmanageable proportions.

On the periphery of the teaching staff is the caretaker. He is disliked by the long-term teachers, and in particular by the Vice-Principal, for the esteem in which he is held by the community is anomalous with his formally low status in the school. He is not, the long-term teachers say, a *real* janitor. He has inherited a house larger than any inhabited by a Colander High teacher and only a physical disability has reduced him to the role of caretaker. The tiro who is observed hobnobbing with him is promptly reprimanded by the Vice-Principal. While the long-term teachers dislike him, they handle him gingerly, for they know that he can make life difficult for them. He can work to rule and neglect to perform services which, while almost indispensable to the smooth running of the school, he is not bound to perform in terms of his contract – answering the telephone, making tea, replenishing supplies of chalk, and so forth. So, while he is quite devoid of formal powers over teachers and scholars, he is nevertheless redoubtable.

His is a strategic position in the school's communication network. 'I am,' he claims justifiably, 'in rather a good position: the Principal tells me things, I see the staff; and the kids tell me things: I get it from all three sides.' Of particular significance is his intimate knowledge of the children. Children gather about him in the playground, come to him with broken pencils and cut fingers, and some, from hungry homes, even breakfast with him at school and are fed on biscuits and the cat's meat [*sic*]. He is, in fact, the only adult in the school with whom the children communicate freely. He knows who broke up the hockey game with studded belts, and why. He knows who made whom pregnant. He knows, in fine, the answers to many questions which the teachers find unfathomable, the solution to many problems teachers find intractable. With him as an ally and confidant a teacher need not go in fear of the unknown: he will, so to speak, know what the natives are saying.

To sum up, the informal organization at Colander High does not coincide with the formal chain of command as laid down in the Education

Ordinance, and this incongruence can be related to factors that stem from the teaching staff's relationship with the community they serve. The Principal, afflicted with working-class and pass-White scholars, is unable to earn the school a 'good name', attracts the enmity of parents and bureaucrats, and loses the respect of his staff. The Vice-Principal is disgruntled because his merited promotion out of the school is thwarted by anti-Catholicism; and he snipes at the authority of the Principal, while shoring up his own. The caretaker is the confidant of the children, and so plays a strategic role in the school's communication network. Thus, the Principal is overshadowed by his Vice-Principal, conflict is endemic between the two; and the caretaker possesses extraordinary authority.

NOTES

1 M. Gluckman, *Custom and Conflict in Africa*, Oxford, Basil Blackwell, 1960, p. 53.

2 M. Gluckman, *ibid.*, p. 27.

3 G. Homans, *The Human Group*, London, Routledge and Kegan Paul, 1951, p. 141.

4 Not merely a matter of boycotting the school, for, as Brian Jackson points out in *An Education System in Miniature* (London, Routledge and Kegan Paul, 1964, p. 88), the parents of English C-stream children often do not come to open days because '. . . having had little education in their own childhood, they felt uncomfortable about presenting themselves at a school, or failed to realize the importance of this personal contact, or were quite unpractised in this kind of social relationship'.

5 B. Berelson and G. Steiner, *Human Behavior: An Inventory of Scientific Findings*, New York, Harcourt, Brace and World, 1964, p. 377.

6 For an illuminating examination of strategies, such as 'secrecy' and 'lying', commonly utilized in some schools 'in order to preserve the face-to-face formalities and prevent incipient interpersonal breakdowns from crystalizing', see R. G. Corwin, *A Sociology of Education*, New York, Appleton-Century-Crofts, 1965, Ch. 10.

Chapter Nine

IN CONCLUSION

Eccentricities of the social structure of Colander High School – such as friction between teachers and pupils, the pre-eminence of the class as a unit of social organization, the rapid turnover of recruits, the remarkable cleavage between long-term teachers and tiros, the former's propensity to seek scapegoats, conflict between the Principal and the Vice-Principal, and the low regard in which the Principal is held by his staff – are related to environmental pressures; that is, to the conflicting demands of government, community, and teachers.

Disaccord concerning the goals of vocational and regulatory training, and the means whereby these goals are to be attained, is endemic to the school. Disciplinary problems ensue, the school's extra-curriculum withers away, and the school class – the members of which owe no allegiance to Houses, forms, clubs, or societies such as might cut across their allegiance to the class – becomes the pre-eminent unit of social structure in the school. Teachers deprived of the means *par excellence* of dividing and ruling their pupils (the creation and manipulation of cross-cutting allegiances) face in class a solidary body of pupils united in their opposition to middle-class adult authority. This increases the difficulty which teachers encounter in maintaining classroom order and diminishes their opportunity of ridding the school of its 'bad name'.

Difficulty is experienced in attracting recruits to the teaching staff and in moderating their rate of turnover. Teachers who have remained for many years have not done so willingly: their desire for promotion out of the school is balked by various circumstances, among the more important of which is their lengthy association with Colander High. These veteran teachers are no less embarrassed by their connection with the school than are tiros, but they are stuck with it and have to make do. They reduce dissonance by being 'loyal' to the school and to Colander: they do not make the kind of disparaging remarks about the school or community that tiros make. They give vent to their frustration in continual scapegoating activity, and exemplify a category of groups (i.e. those which face amorphous, continuing, inescapable, and apparently intractable frustrations) which takes its place alongside other categories such as 'struggle groups' described by scholars (e.g. Coser) as exhibiting a perennial need for scapegoating.

The Principal and Vice-Principal contend for ascendancy over the staff. They are drawn into competition by their need to win the approval of school inspectors and others if they are to secure promotion out of Colander High. Their competition is rendered all the more keen by the strength of the Vice-Principal's desire to be quit of the school. Increasing the Vice-Principal's temptation to compete is his superior's manifest vulnerability. Not only does the Principal lack the social skills necessary to cope successfully with a formidable Vice-Principal, but his status as *middle man* is particularly onerous (for he is unable to reconcile conflicting pressures and earns the enmity of community and bureaucracy alike) so that he forfeits the respect of his staff and is unable to call upon them for support in rivalry with his subordinate.

Principal and Vice-Principal confront each other with smouldering hostility; veterans fretfully pick over the inadequacies of tiros; teachers provoke their pupils with a mixture of aloof indifference and exasperation; children respond with defiance and incomprehension. This demoralization and dissension have their roots not in individual psychology (for the teachers and children of Colander High are neither more unreasonable nor less sweet-natured than the common run of humanity) but in the social situation. Demoralization and dissension are consequences of the conjunction in the school of contrary forces immanent in the society of which the school is a part.

Much conflict centres upon teachers' attempts to force their bewildered pupils to conform to middle-class expectations. The presence of pass-Whites among the children intensifies teachers' distaste for their work and so adds piquancy to the prevailing antipathy. Passing merely exacerbates this antipathy without altering its nature. It does, however, involve the school in strains of another kind.

Pass-Whites are enrolled at Colander High partly because they have been sent there by the School Board. School Boards in Cape Town were for many decades in the perplexing position of being required to carry out the instructions of the Provincial Department of Education to the effect that all White children must be accommodated in White schools and that all White schools must be reserved for the exclusive use of White children, while not being provided with criteria whereby they might readily differentiate all White children from all non-White children. To establish the racial status of ambiguously White children involves recourse to cumbersome and offensive procedures the results of which were often contentious and which rarely failed to aggrieve either the children or the Principals of the schools to which they were sent. In the attempt to avoid involving themselves in incommodious disputes School Boards set up schools specially to cater for 'better-class borderline pupils'. This strategem was denied them by the Department, who reclassified as Coloured a number of putatively White 'buffer schools'. School Boards thereafter adopted the alternative course of gently guiding marginally White children to those *de facto* 'buffer schools' which were prepared to accept them. One such school is Colander High.

Pass-Whites are enrolled at Colander High also because the Principal needs them. If he were to enrol only those pupils whose Whiteness is unassailable, then his enrolment, already in rapid decline, would drop to the point where the continued employment of all his present staff could not be justified and the very existence of the school would be endangered.

Pass-Whites are in the school also because the White people of Colander need them in order to keep their school afloat. If the school were to sink there would be one less (and a very significant one less) White organization in Colander. Colander's claim to White estate would then meet with even more scepticism than is already customary.

Pass-Whites are in the school also because that is where they want to be. Entry to a White school is a momentous advance for those bent on passing. They find in White schools one of the selected and segmentary roles necessary for their purpose.

So it is that the presence of pass-Whites at Colander High affords demonstrable benefits to diverse sections of the populace. The contemplation of this fact does not, however, give rise to general satisfaction. On the contrary, the presence of pass-Whites offends against popular notions of racial propriety, reduces to futility all attempts to win for the school a reputation of respectability, imperils teachers' opportunities for occupational advancement, places in question the precarious White status of many in the school, and thus occasions much alarm and distress.

Pass-Whites are welcome in the school in that according to one set of – public – criteria they are White, or at least not officially not White, and so can be used to sustain the school's failing enrolment. They are unwelcome in that according to another set of – private – criteria they are not White, or at least no more than questionably White, and so compromise by contamination the school's White status.

1*

They are both White and not White at the same time. They are in a White school and therefore they 'must' be White: the law is witness to that. Yet 'everybody' knows that they are not White, not really. They are something in between. But the law, which is an ass, knows no in-betweenness. It dichotomizes inflexibly, imposing a clumsy disjunction upon the subtly variegated flux of reality.

It is the lack of correspondence between public and private criteria of racial status that the Principal exploits in the attempt to observe his minimal professional obligations of maintaining both his school's enrolment and its White identity. If there were close correspondence between public and private criteria then he would probably either have to close his school for lack of White pupils or have it relegated to Coloured status – and in either event suffer professional degradation.

The self-same lack of correspondence is the source of many of his troubles. He cannot maintain enrolment without recruiting marginally White children who endanger the schools' officially White status, and he cannot safeguard White status without sacrificing enrolment. For there comes a point at which bureaucrats take official cognizance of the unofficial reputation of a 'buffer school' and reclassify it as Coloured.

Pass-Whites too exploit the lack of correspondence between public and private criteria of racial status. It is the law's intolerance of racial ambiguity (together with Colander's relative indifference to that ambiguity) which makes it possible for in-betweens to become officially White: if the law were to countenance a category of In-Betweens then pass-Whites would probably be In-Betweens and not Whites.

So the inflexibility of apartheid laws is, up to a point, self-defeating. Laws embodying a rigid dichotomy of White and non-White which are intended to create an impassable barrier to upward mobility between the races act both as an incentive to mobility and as a means whereby it might be consummated. The irony cannot be altogether evaded by recognizing in law a category of In-Betweens, for that would merely beget a class in between the Whites and the In-Betweens, and then another in between *them* . . . and so on until the law reflects not the disjunction which is the essence of apartheid but the flowing together of White and Coloured apparent in Colander.

In sum, the dissension and demoralization which bedevil Colander High are manifestations of larger conflicts between a working class who wish to be themselves and a teaching profession bent on elevating them, and between a community who regard passing as commonplace and venial and administrators who pronounce it unlawful and abominable.

Appendix A

SOCIO-ECONOMIC CLASSIFICATION OF THE OCCUPATIONS OF PARENTS OF COLANDER HIGH SCHOOL PUPILS

The socio-economic classification of occupations used here is one adapted to local conditions by E. Batson.[1]

A   Administrative and independent professional (e.g. accountant).
B   Subordinate professional and independent commercial (e.g. independent electrician).
C   Subordinate commercial (e.g. telephonist).
D   Skilled manual (e.g. cable-joiner).
E   Predominantly manual, but involving special responsibility (e.g. engine driver).
F   Semi-skilled manual (e.g. postal clerk).
G   Unskilled manual (e.g. porter).
H   Occupations not actively directed towards getting an income (e.g. pensioner).
J   Seeking employment.

Of the 170 responses to a questionnaire administered to pupils of Colander, 158 proved sufficient for purposes of classification. Of the 135 fathers or male guardians concerned:

51 (37·8%) pursued occupations which fall into group F
40 (29·6%) pursued occupations which fall into group D
17 (12·6%) pursued occupations which fall into group E
12   pursued occupations which fall into group C
6   pursued occupations which fall into group B
6   pursued occupations which fall into group H
2   pursued occupations which fall into group G
1   pursued occupations which fall into group A

Of the 23 mothers reported as being employed:

17 (73·9%) pursued occupations which fall into group F
3   pursued occupations which fall into group E
2   pursued occupations which fall into group C
1   pursued occupations which fall into group B

Appendix B

QUESTIONNAIRE ADMINISTERED TO PUPILS OF COLANDER HIGH SCHOOL

Do not write your name or address on this paper. Your answers will be kept secret. Your parents and teachers will not see what you have written.

DATE OF BIRTH
SEX
CLASS

I. a. Who usually stays at your home? UNDERLINE THE RIGHT NAMES

My mother	My brother-s (Say how many)
My father	My sister-s (Say how many)
My step-mother	My brother-s-in-law (Say how many)
My step-father	My sister-s-in-law (Say how many)
My grandmother-s	My sister-s child-ren (Say how many)
(Say how many)	My brother-s child-ren (Say how many)
My grandfather-s	My aunt-s child-ren (Say how many)
(Say how many)	My uncle-s child-ren (Say how many)
(My uncle-s (Say how many)	
My aunt-s (Say how many)	

b. Perhaps there are some other people staying with you, such as other relatives, or boarders, or just friends. Say who they are. Do not give their names, like Mary or John, but say what kind of people they are, like boarder or friend.

II. a. Who, if anybody, speaks more Afrikaans than English at home?
b. Who, if anybody, speaks more of any other language than they speak English or Afrikaans? What language do they speak?

III. a. Who looks after you at home?
b. Do you ever look after your younger brothers or sisters? Say YES or NO.
c. Do any of your older brothers or sisters ever look after you? Say YES or NO.

IV. a. Do you get pocket money?
b. Who gives it to you?

V. What kind of work do your parents or guardians do?
VI. a. When you finish school what kind of work would you really like to do?

b. What kind of work do you think you really will do when you leave school?

c. What kind of work do your parents or guardians want you to do?

d. Have any of your teachers ever said what kind of work they think you should do when you leave school?

e. If so, what kind of work do they think you should do?

f. What are some kinds of work you would definitely not like?

g. Why?

VII.a. At what age would you like to leave school?

b. At what age do your parents or guardians want you to leave school?

VIII. UNDERLINE THE RIGHT ANSWER-S
When I leave school I shall
get a job
stay and help at home
go to technical college
go to university

NOTES

1 E. Batson, *Occupational Classification (S.S.8)*, manuscript issued by Department of Social Science, University of Cape Town, undated.

References

ABEL, T., 'The Operation Called Verstehen', *American Journal of Sociology*, November 1948, pp. 211–18.

ALEXANDER, R., and H. J. SIMONS, *Job Reservation and the Trade Unions*, Cape Town, Enterprise Press, 1959.

ALLPORT, G. W., *The Nature of Prejudice*, New York, Doubleday, 1958.

ANDRESKI, S., *The Uses of Comparative Sociology*, Berkeley, University of California Press, 1964.

ANON., 'The Origin and Incidence of Miscegenation at the Cape During the Dutch East India Company's Regime 1652–1795', *Race Relations Journal*, Vol. XX, No. 2, 1953, pp. 23–7.

BANTON, M., *Race Relations*, London, Tavistock Publications; New York, Basic Books, 1967.

BATSON, E., *Occupational Classification*, School of Social Science, University of Cape Town, undated.

BERELSON, B., and G. STEINER, *Human Behavior: An Inventory of Scientific Findings*, New York, Harcourt, Brace and World, 1964.

BERRY, B., *Almost White*, New York, Macmillan, 1963.

BETTELHEIM, B., and J. JANOWITZ, *Social Change amd Prejudice*, Glencoe, Ill., The Free Press, 1950.

BIDWELL, C. E., 'The School as a Formal Organization', in J. G. March (ed.) *Handbook of Organizations*, Chicago, Rand McNally, 1965, pp. 972–1022.

BLAU, P. M., and W. R. SCOTT, *Formal Organizations*, San Francisco, Chandler, 1962.

BUNTING, B., *The Rise of the South African Reich*, Harmondsworth, Penguin, 1964.

The *Cape Argus*, Cape Town, daily newspaper.

The *Cape Times*, Cape Town, daily newspaper.

CARSTENS, W. P., *The Social Structure of a Cape Coloured Reserve*, London, Oxford University Press, 1966.

CHARTERS, W. W., and N. L. GAGE (eds.) *Readings in the Social Psychology of Education*, Boston, Allyn and Bacon, 1963.

CILLIERS, S. P., *The Coloured People of South Africa*, Cape Town, Banier, 1963.

COLE, M., *South Africa*, New York, Dutton, 1961.

CONNOLLY, C., *Enemies of Promise*, London, Routledge and Kegan Paul, 1949.

CORWIN, R. G., *A Sociology of Education*, New York, Appleton-Century-Crofts, 1965.

COSER, L., *The Functions of Social Conflict*, London, Routledge and Kegan Paul, 1995.

DAVIS, J. A. M., 'Secondary Schools as Communities', *Educational Review,* Vol. 9, No. 3, 1957, pp. 179–89.

DICKIE-CLARKE, H. F. *The Marginal Situation*, London, Routledge and Kegan Paul, 1966.

DORNBUSCH, S. M., 'The Military Academy as an Assimilating Institution', *Social Forces*, Vol. 33, pp. 316–21.

DOVER, C., *Half-Caste*, London, Secker and Warburg, 1937.

DOXEY, G. V., *The Industrial Colour Bar in South Africa*, London, Oxford University Press, 1961.

DRAKE, S., and H. R. CAYTON, *Black Metropolis*, New York, Harper and Row, 1962.

EELLS, K., *et al.*, *Intelligence and Cultural Differences*, Chicago, University of Chicago Press, 1951.

ETZIONI, A., *A Comparative Analysis of Complex Organizations*, Glencoe, Ill., The Free Press, 1961.

FINDLAY, G., *Miscegenation*, Pretoria, Pretoria News Publishers, 1936.

FLOUD, J. E., A. H. HALSEY and F. M. MARTIN, *Social Class and Educational Opportunity*, London, William Heinemann, 1956.

FLOUD, J. E., and A. H. HALSEY, *The Sociology of Education*, Oxford, Blackwell, 1958.

FOWLER, C. de K., *School Administration*, Cape Town, Maskew Miller, 1953.

FUGARD, A., *The Blood Knot*, Cape Town, Simondium Publishers, 1964.

GARDINER, P. (ed.), *Theories of History*, New York, The Free Press, 1964.

GLUCKMAN, M., *Custom and Conflict in Africa*, Oxford, Basil Blackwell, 1960.

GOFFMAN, E., *The Presentation of Self in Everyday Life*, New York, Doubleday, 1959.

GORDON, W., 'The Role of the Teacher in the Social Structure of the High School', *Journal of Educational Sociology*, Vol. 29, Sept. 1955, pp. 21–9.

GREEN, L. G., *Grow Lovely, Growing Old*, Cape Town, Timmins, 1951.

GREENE, G. (ed.), *The Old School*, London, Jonathan Cape, 1934.

HAUSKNECHT, M., *The Joiners*, New York, The Bedminster Press, 1962.

HOETINK, H., *Two Variants in Caribbean Race Relations*, London, Oxford University Press, 1967.

HOMANS, G., *The Human Group*, London, Routledge and Kegan Paul, 1951.

HORRELL, M, *Race Classification in South Africa – Its Effects on Human Beings*, Johannesburg, South African Institute of Race Relations, 1958.

HUNTER, E., *Blackboard Jungle*, New York, Simon and Schuster, 1954.

JACKSON, B., *An Education System in Miniature*, London, Routledge and Kegan Paul, 1964.

JARVIE, I., *The Revolution in Anthropology*, New York, Humanities Press, 1964.

JEFFRYS, M., 'Where do Coloureds come from?', *Drum*, Nos. 102–106, and 108, 1959.

KERR, M., *The People of Ship Street*, London, Routledge and Kegan Paul, 1958.

KIES, B. M., *The Policy of Educational Segregation and Some of its Effects Upon the Coloured People of the Cape*, unpublished thesis, University of Cape Town, 1946.

KUPER, L., *Living in Towns*, London, Cresset, 1953.

LAIDLAW, P. W., *The Growth of Government of Cape Town*, Cape Town, Unie Volks Pers, 1939.

Lovedale Past and Present, Lovedale, South Africa, Mission Press, 1887.

LYND, R. S., and H. M. LYND, *Middletown: A Study in American Culture*, New York, Harcourt, Brace and World, 1929.

MACCRONE, I. D., *Race Attitudes in South Africa*, Johannesburg, Witwatersrand University Press, 1957.

MCKERRON, M. E., *A History of Education in South Africa*, Pretoria, Von Schaik, 1934.

MALHERBE, E. G., *Education in South Africa*, Cape Town, Juta, 1925.

MARAIS, J. S., *The Cape Coloured People*, Johannesburg, Witwatersrand University Press, 1957.

MARCH, J. G. (ed.), *Handbook of Organizations*, Chicago, Rand McNally, 1965.

MARQUARD, L., *The Peoples and Policies of South Africa*, London, Oxford University Press, 1962.

MAYER, P., 'Witchcraft', Inaugural Lecture to the Rhodes University, Grahamstown, South Africa, 1954.

MERTON, R. K., *Social Theory and Social Structure*, New York, The Free Press, 1965.

MILLIN, S. G., *God's Stepchildren*, London, Constable, 1924.

—— *The People of South Africa*, New York, Knopf, 1954.

MYRDAL, G., *An American Dilemma*, New York, Harper, 1944.

Outspan, 17 Nov. 1950.

PARSONS, T., *Religious Perspectives of College Teaching in Sociology and Social Psychology*, New Haven, The Edward W. Hagen Foundation, 1951.

PATTERSON, S., *Colour and Culture in South Africa*, London, Routledge and Kegan Paul, 1953.

PELLS, E. G., *300 Years of Education in South Africa*, Cape Town, Juta, 1954.

PIERSON, D., *Negroes in Brazil*, Chicago, University of Chicago Press, 1942.

POPPER, K., *The Open Society and its Enemies*, New York, Harper and Row, 1963.

PRINGLE, J. D., 'The British Commune', *Encounter*, Vol. 26, No. 2, 1961, pp. 24-8.

ROGERS, C. A., and C. FRANTZ, *Racial Themes in Southern Rhodesia*, New Haven, Yale University Press, 1962.

SHEPHERD, R. W. H., 'Mixed Schooling in South African History', in *Cape Times*, 27 Feb. 1958.

SPINLEY, B. M., *The Deprived and the Privileged*, London, Routledge and Kegan Paul, 1953.

STONEQUIST, E. V. S., *The Marginal Man*, New York, Russell and Russell, 1961.

TOWNSEND, J., *The Young Devils*, London, Chatto and Windus, 1958.

TUCKER, W., 'Max Weber's Verstehen', *The Sociological Quarterly*, Spring 1965, pp. 157-65.

VAN DEN BERGHE, P., *South Africa: A Study in Conflict*, Middletown, Wesleyan University Press, 1965.

—— *Caneville: The Social Structure of a South African Town*, Middletown, Wesleyan University Press, 1964.

VAN DER MERWE, H. W., *Social Stratification in a Cape Coloured Community*, M.A. Thesis, University of Stellenbosch, 1957.

VANDER ZANDEN, J. W., *American Minority Relations* (second edition), New York, The Ronald Press Co., 1966.

WALLER, W. W., *The Sociology of Teaching*, New York, John Wiley, 1932.

WATKINS, J., 'Historical Explanation in the Social Sciences', in P. Gardiner (ed.) *Theories of History*, New York, The Free Press, 1964.

WATSON, G., 'The Process of Passing for White in South Africa: A Study in Cumulative Ad Hoc-ery', *The Canadian Review of Sociology and Anthropology*, Vol. 4, No. 3, pp. 141-7.

WAUGH, A., *The Loom of Youth*, London, Grant Richards, 1918.

WEBB, J., 'The Sociology of a School', *British Journal of Sociology*, Vol. 13, No. 3, 1962, pp. 264-72.

WEBER, M., *The Theory of Social and Economic Organization*, New York, The Free Press, 1964.

WEINBERG, I., *The English Public Schools*, New York, Atherton Press, 1967.

WILKINSON, R., *The Prefects*, London, Oxford University Press, 1964.

WILLIAMS, R. M., Jr., *The Reduction of Intergroup Tensions*, New York, Social Science Research Council, 1943.

WILSON, J., *Public Schools and Private Practice*, London, Allen and Unwin, 1962.

YOUNG, M., and P. WILLMOTT, *Family and Kinship in East London*, London, Routledge and Kegan Paul, 1957.

OFFICIAL REPORTS, BLUE BOOKS, SELECT DOCUMENTS

Annual Report[s] of the Cape School Board.

Cape of Good Hope: Annexures to Votes and Proceedings of the Legislative Council for 1865.

Cape of Good Hope Education Commission, 1912 [CP 6–1912.]

Education Commission, 1861 (Cape of Good Hope) [G.24–63].

Education Commission, 1892: First Report and Third Report [G. 9–91].

Education Gazette.

Hansard.

Minutes of the Cape School Board.

Population Census 1960: Sample Tabulations, Nos. 2 and 4, Pretoria, The Government Printer.

Records of the Provincial Council.

Report of the Commission of the Cape Coloured Population of the Union, Pretoria, The Government Printer, 1937 [U.G. 45/1937].

Report of the Interdepartmental Committee on Native Education, Pretoria, The Government Printer, 1935 [U.G. 29/1936].

Report[s] of the Superintendent-General of Education [Cape Province.]

ROSS, D., *Preliminary Report on the State of Education in the Cape of Good Hope,* 1883 [G. 12–83].

Author Index

Subject Index

Afrikaans accent, 82

Afrikaans language, social unacceptability of, 7–10, 18

Anglican Synod of the Diocese of Cape Town, 30

apartheid, ix, xiii, xiv, 17, 22, 53, 55, 114

association, as test for European status, 41–2

Bantu, 3, 4

'borderline cases', 34, 40, 48, 53, 57–9, 113

'buffer' schools
in Cape Province, 34, 57–8
Colander High as, 40, 52, 113

Cape Coloured Commission, 14, 17

Cape of Good Hope Education Commission, 1912, 38

Cape Provincial Department of Education, 33, 40ff

Cape School Board, 34–7, 40–48, 53, 58, 61

caretaker, the, of Colander High School
authority in school organization, 80, 109–10
conflict with Vice-Principal, 103, 108

churches
attendance at, as part of pass-White process, 60
division of responsibility with state for schools, 29

liberal attitude of English churches, 30, 37

Mission Schools, 30–2
see also Dutch Reformed Church

class, see social class

classes
as unit of school social structure, 68–9, 72, 77

Colander
attraction of, to Coloured migrants, 23
geography of, 1–2

Colander High School
admission methods, 40–2, 46–7
admission refusals, 43, 53
as 'buffer school', 40, 52, 113
compared with English Public School, 67ff.
large number of pass-White pupils at, 50–1
organization of standards and classes, 69–72
poor reputation of, 82–4
racial reclassification, fears for, 49, 114

Colander High School Committee
apathy of, 106
disagreement on race classification, 43–7
part in admission of pass-White pupils, 51–2
responsibility for admission of pupils, 40, 42